GUIDE TO MAKING FIRE WITHOUT MATCHES

GUIDE TO MAKING FIRE WITHOUT MATCHES

tips, tactics, and techniques for Starting a fire in any Situation

CHRISTOPHER NYERGES
FOREWORD BY AL CORNELL

Skyhorse Publishing

Skyhorse Publishing books may be purchased in bulk at special discounts for sales promotion, corporate gifts, fund-raising, or educational purposes. Special editions can also be created to specifications. For details, contact the Special Sales Department, Skyhorse Publishing, 307 West 36th Street, 11th Floor, New York, NY 10018 or info@skyhorsepublishing.com.

Skyhorse® and Skyhorse Publishing® are registered trademarks of Skyhorse Publishing, Inc.®, a Delaware corporation.

Visit our website at www.skyhorsepublishing.com.

10 9 8 7 6 5 4 3 2

Library of Congress Cataloging-in-Publication Data is available on file.

Cover design by Tom Lau
Cover illustration credit: iStockphoto

All photographs and illustrations in this book are courtesy of the author, unless otherwise noted.

Print ISBN: 978-1-5107-4989-4
Ebook ISBN: 978-1-5107-4991-7

Printed in China

Larry Dean Olsen's *Outdoor Survival Skills* book was my first serious introduction to the world of fire. Through his book, he was my tutor for fire by the bow and drill. Though we had phone conversations, and shared e-mails, when I was the editor of *Wilderness Way* magazine, I regret that we never met in person. Larry was perhaps the singular individual who kept alive the primitive technologies when no one else was interested.

It is to Larry Dean Olsen, and his memory, that I dedicate this book.

TABLE OF CONTENTS

ACKNOWLEDGMENTS

I want to thank and acknowledge everyone who assisted in some way with this book, and those who walked with me on the Fire Path. Thank you Gary Gonzales, Piero del Valle, Daniela del Valle, Alan Halcon, Dude McLean, Rick Adams (who has many photos in this book), Carlos Hall, Al Cornell, Paul Campbell, Steve Watts, Jim Robertson, Keith Farrar, James Ruther, Enrique Villasenor, Nachshon Rose, Helen, and everyone else who taught me something along the way, whose names I may have never known . . .

FOREWORD

BY AL CORNELL

Fire: It's the *main* reason we as modern humans are here, and exist as we do today.

For our prehistoric ancestors, it was the center of their lives. Early hominids who learned to use it evolved; those who didn't, disappeared.

Its importance in prehistoric and early historic times became so recognized that it also became highly "ceremonial." From Egyptians and Romans to the American Indians of today, the starting of a ceremonial fire signaled the beginning of an important event, be it military or tribal.

In our modern societies we still use fire as the symbol of the initiation of important events, such as the Olympic Games and as eternal flames to show reverence to historical sites and personages like the Tomb of the Unknown Soldier and the grave site of President Kennedy, both at Arlington cemetery.

Although fire in the lives of humans today plays hundreds of invaluable roles, these roles have become secondary—all but ignored—as we go about our daily routines. However, fire can quickly become of utmost importance when we find ourselves away from our urban environments and back in nature. Wilderness enthusiasts, such as hikers, hunters, and backpackers, recognize the importance fire represents in a cold-weather survival emergency and will—with the major support of fire—live through such difficult challenges. Fire can become the big "mitigater" when we make life-threatening mistakes in the woods. However, those who venture outdoors and choose to take a cavalier approach toward fire's potential life-saving role may someday be carried out of a forest in a "deceased" recovery operation.

Therefore the importance of learning all about how to use fire to make the wilderness experience both enjoyable and safe cannot be overstated. The more knowledge and experience modern peoples acquire about fire—especially the prehistoric methods—the more adapted and confident they become about spending time outdoors. Even during times of benign weather, fire makes outdoor life so much more enjoyable, especially with the morning coffee, cooking meals, and the nighttime social fire. And, the experience is further enhanced when the fire is started with, for example, a bow drill, creating an ember, and then with some tinder, slowly blowing that ember in order to give birth to fire.

Learning outdoor skills, such as erecting a shelter, is empowering. But learning to make fire from materials collected in nature is absolutely transforming.

We should all learn these outdoor fire skills: pioneer fire skills, as well as prehistoric fire skills. Armed with this knowledge, we will never be the same. It literally will transform us!

And then, fire forever ties us to our prehistoric ancestry.

ABOUT AL CORNELL:

Cornell was one of the teachers of the author of this book. Cornell, born and raised in Central California, entered the US Army as a Second Lieutenant and became an Army helicopter pilot. He served on active duty for thirty years, spending seventeen years overseas in four Latin American countries and two Asian countries, including two tours in Vietnam as a helicopter pilot. Cornell and spouse retired to Sedona, Arizona, in 1994, and among other volunteer activities, such as Search and Rescue, he teaches a variety of wilderness skills and prehistoric skills, focusing on wilderness safety and preparedness. He and his teaching partner Michael Campbell teach fire-starting for survival several times a year at SAR (Search and Rescue) Basic Training.

Al Cornell, from left, author Nyerges, and Michael Campbell. (photographer unknown).

INTRODUCTION

I have always been fascinated by fire. As the other frivolous novelties of youth came and went, there was always fire.

As a child, I would sit by the fireplace and watch the flames as they consumed wood. I loved the look, the smell, the sound of fire. Something about its unique qualities captured my attention.

As a young child, I would play with matches and watch each match scratch to a flame, and then I would hold it as long as I could before it would start to burn my fingers and I would blow it out.

As a teen, a campout was not a campout without a fire. It was the central organizing force of any group on any outdoor excursion. We sat around the fire and talked, and sang, and ate, and stared into the dazzling light show that both warmed us and lit our night. We'd even sit around a large campfire in a light rain, because the fire made us so much more comfortable, and would dry us about as quickly as we got wet.

As a young adult, I read about Native Americans of the Plains, and how they were masters of their environment, and I marveled at their ability to eke fire from wood. I knew that to be the masters of your environment, you had to have a broad and intimate knowledge of plants—plants for food, medicine, soap, fiber, and yes, for the tools for making fire.

Eventually, I obtained a copy of Larry Dean Olsen's *Outdoor Survival Skills* book from my older brother, and I began to practice making fire with pieces of wood that I collected and shaped into a bow, a drill, and a baseplate. I practiced obsessively, but only produced smoke, and never an ember. After a few hundred attempts, finally, one day I succeeded in creating an ember from my own muscle-power and carefully shaped pieces of wood. I have never forgotten that day. I felt as if I had graduated from some long apprenticeship into the mastery of fire. On that day, when I moved into the black-belt status of fire-making, my life-long study of fire took on a new quality. I was no longer a child playing with fire. I was now a teacher and protector of the sacred fire.

I am not the only one who has been fascinated by fire.

Fire—what it is and what it represents—has figured prominently in various religions, and in their mythoses. This is not surprising when we consider the prominence of fire as a key factor in the very development of what we call civilization. The wide use of fire allowed technologies to arise, which allowed mankind the time and luxury to expand our minds to fuller potentials.

I hope you enjoy this book, and benefit from the many lessons here. I hope this inspires you to see fire as much more than a mundane force of nature. I hope you too recognize fire as the great unifier, the great power, that semi-mysterious force that has helped us to unlock so many of life's most profound mysteries.

Nyerges (center at table) conducts a Fire Workshop where all the methods discussed in this book are discussed and practiced. Photo by Rick Adams

CHAPTER 1

FIRE AT THE VERY ROOT OF CIVILIZATION AND CULTURE

Fire is so basic and fundamental to our daily life that we barely think about it anymore. We believe we've mastered it . . . after all, it's everywhere hidden in plain view in our modern life. It's in the car that drives us. It's in the wall heater that warms the home. It's in the stove that cooks our food, and the food at all restaurants. It's in the light bulbs that light our world—yes, it is! Its latent force is in the butane lighter that we carry around in our pockets. It's everywhere.

When you read survival literature and watch survival movies, you're likely to see the obvious importance of fire. It's always there.

Fire is one of the most basic neccssities of survival. Along with water and oxygen, fire is right up there as part of that Holy Trinity.

In *Lord of the Flies,* fire was there, playing an obviously important role. In *Quest for Fire*, fire was the goal to be obtained, though it was a fanciful and historically very inaccurate movie.

As we study ancient civilizations, we realize that when life was very basic, everyone needed food, water, and tools. Fire was always there, to cook the food, to purify the water, to make the tools. The ancient Egyptians drew pictures of their fire tools on their walls, along with every other aspect of their lives, so we know that they used a variation of the bow and drill, which we simply call the Egyptian bow-drill. The Anasazi, who lived in the American desert Southwest, created a culture of adobe and rock cliff homes, irrigation ditches, pottery, fabric, and agriculture. Of course, fire was everywhere—the fragments of drills and hearths are still found in the remote cliff dwellings, as well as evidence of a system of communication by fire.

Fire goes back to the earliest unrecorded lives of the first humans. It's essential to human life as we know it.

ISHI'S LESSON

Historical picture of Ishi with his hand drill.

In 1911, an approximately fifty-year-old Native American walked out of the forest into the little town of Oroville, near the foothills of Lassen Peak in Northern California. He had survived in the wild, the last of his tribe, and now he was alone. Once it was clear who this man was, anthropologists came from far and wide to study this living window into the past.

Among other things, he shared his method of making fire, probably the most widely practiced method of friction fire-making throughout world history. The details have been recorded by Theodora Kroeber in *Ishi in Two Worlds*.

According to Kroeber, "The drill, or upper piece, is an ordinary round stick of a size to fit the hearth socket, about the length of an arrow shaft, but larger at one end. Ishi preferred buckeye for his drills, but sage brush, poison oak, or indeed any fairly hard wood will answer equally well."

Kroeber describes how Ishi placed various tinders around the notch in the hearth board, and how Ishi squatted when spinning the drill. Ishi had to rapidly spin the drill between his hands, and when his hands came to the bottom of the drill, he had to rapidly bring them up to the top of the drill, and begin spinning again. As Ishi spun, more and more sawdust appeared in the notch.

Kroeber goes on to point out that this process is something that is only mastered by experience, and that great patience and delicate control are required.

The best source of historical information about Ishi was recorded in Theodora Kroeber's Ishi in Two Worlds.

TODAY

Technologically, we've come a long way from the days of Ishi. Yet, despite all our advances, we are still surrounded by fire. We still need it, for it gives us light, and life, and food, and warmth. Fire is in our stove, though we barely see it. It's in the heater that warms our home, hidden. It's in our car's engine, beyond our peering eyes.

Our life is better because of fire, and its many benefits cannot be overstated. It has been with us from the very beginning, and will be with us to the very end.

QUIZ

1. How was fire made in *Lord of the Flies*?
2. Who was Ishi?
3. How did Ishi make fire?

ANSWERS

1. Piggy's "specs" (eye glasses).
2. Ishi was the last "wild" Indian who came out of the wild, in 1911 in Northern California.
3. Ishi made fire with a hand drill, which he taught to anthropologist Kroeber.

ACTION:

If you have not already seen it, watch the original *Lord of the Flies* movie from 1963.

SMOKE SIGNALS:

"Fire, one of the most important forces of nature, is a truly valued resource. But be careful—it can have both positive and negative impacts since fire can both help and harm you. Fire provides heat and light, which is necessary to sustain and regenerate life. But it can also be very destructive and can damage anything in its path in the blink of an eye."—*Struggle for Survival: Fire*, Christine Dugan

CHAPTER 2

CONSIDERATIONS IN BUILDING THE FIRE

WHY BUILD A FIRE?

Fire warms us. It cooks our food. It purifies our water. It lights up the night. It allows us to signal over long distances.

Fire has served a role in the making of our tools, whether it's the fire-hardening of a digging stick, or the quenching of a sword or knife in the works. It's used to fire pottery so that the pots will hold water and be usable for cooking. It was used to clear fields so that they would be usable for agriculture. Fire has always been a part of our lives.

Basic fire skills will never "go out of style."

Today, we have no shortage of futuristic fire starters available at any backpacking shop. But even if we possess the best high-tech fire-starting tools, we can still lose them, or use them up. Even the common Bic lighter is a pretty remarkable device, but people misplace them all the time, and they run out of fuel.

The ability to make a fire—with modern or primitive tools—will never go out of style.

Fire has been called "caveman TV."

Have you ever gone on a campout where everyone sat around the fire and talked and sang? It was great, wasn't it? Somehow, the fire in the middle unified everyone, and as they talked and sang, their eyes were always on the fire. The flickering flames would warm the night, dry out wet clothes from the rain, cook a pot of soup or coffee, and somehow in its primal way, make everything good again. It was—and still is—a remarkable substance.

The lack of a fire

If you've ever had a campout and *didn't* have that central fire, it sure made a big difference, didn't it? Maybe it was too wet and your little group simply couldn't get a fire going, so everyone retreated into their tents. Maybe it was a legal issue, as you were camping during the height of a dry, windy fire season. Or maybe you could not afford to be seen during a time of warfare or other hostilities. You got by, but fire could have made your life so much more pleasant, unifying, comforting.

Fire in the rain

Dude McLean of the DirtTime events shared with me his experience during one of his week-long DirtTime educational events, with about a hundred or so campers in Eastern Wyoming. It was June, so everyone expected hot and dry weather, but the first two days brought hard rain. It seemed miserable at first, because everything was done outside.

McLean pointed out that a few of them decided, "Let's make a fire anyway." In the large open area where the fire pit was located, they first created a little bench-like platform so there could be some initial cover from the rain. A fire was built underneath, and it was fed pine needles and bark and bits of paper. It puffed out great clouds of smoke as it dried out the moisture in the wood. I was a bit skeptical, but at least a few of us kept working at this fire, while most of the attendees were safely under cover. After thirty minutes or so, we were able to add branches, and as they caught fire, we were able to add big branches. Gradually a bonfire about five feet across was built. It didn't seem to initially produce much heat because everything was wet. But within another thirty minutes, others saw that the fire was a real concern, and began to collect a semi-mountainous pile of firewood just outside the circle.

The rain continued to fall, of course, and we continued to add wood to the fire strategically. It did eventually provide significant heat, and anyone standing close to this bonfire could fairly quickly dry out from the heat—even as the rain continued!

Though there were some events that occurred elsewhere under cover of a tarp or roof, there was always a good crowd around the fire for those first two days of rain. You still got wet standing there, but you could turn around and around so that you could dry out as soon as you got wet. The fire allowed an otherwise unpleasant and uncomfortable event to become tolerable and challenging.

WHY BUILD A FIRE?

Like with real estate, it's all location, location, location.

Location is important with real estate, and where you build your wilderness shelter. It's also important with fire. Location, location, location.

SAFETY

Safety is your first consideration, over all others. You don't want a fire on thick duff, where an underground fire could smolder for days, and break out somewhere else when you least expect it. The ground should be firm and compact, and there should be no low-hanging overhead branches. Now, there could be an exception to this, such as when you are in hiding or being pursued and you really need a fire, but it cannot be seen. In such a case, you'd still need to consider safety paramount.

To have a low-key fire, you probably will dig a hole first, and keep the fire very small and not smokey. I nearly always dig a hole for every fire I make, and this assumes there is not an already-established fire pit in the area for me to use. This means I have found a safe location that is close, but not too close, to my sleeping area. Ideally, it's in the middle of my camp area.

Never build a fire inside a brush shelter. If anything, you can heat rocks and roll them inside where they will radiate heat. You can see that a fire pit has been built well outside of this simple brush shelter.

In general, it's not a good idea to build a fire in your primitive shelter. If you're in a lean-to or a small brush shelter, well, your shelter is all tinder! You can't risk your whole shelter going up in flames. If you've built much more than a primitive shelter—a large tipi-shaped shelter, or something akin to a log cabin with a high ceiling—you might be able to have a small fire inside, but you still need to be very watchful.

The best choice for heating a primitive shelter is to heat rocks in your fire, outside the shelter. Then, when the rocks are very hot after an hour or so of "cooking," you can roll one or more into a carefully prepared hollow just inside the entry of the shelter. These can give off an amazing amount of heat.

Once, while ten of us from the WTI Survival Training School were camped in the high desert, it was very cold and windy. We dug a hole nearly five feet deep and about three feet across. Yes, that's much deeper than you'd normally need for a campfire, but the winds were strong, and we didn't want to risk embers blowing around and causing a fire. So we dug a very deep fire pit, and then dug our own sleeping holes that radiated out from the fire pit, like the rays of a sunflower. Many years later, I learned to build dug-out body hollow shelters and cover them with a thick roof of branches and leaves. I would then would roll a hot rock into the shelter to stay warm at night. That kept us warm in the desert, out of the wind, and no need for a potentially dangerous fire.

PROXIMITY

Your fire needs to be close to your center of operations, not necessarily close to your shelter. Remember, if you're out camping—especially if it's a primitive situation—your fire area is your kitchen where you'll be doing all your cooking. Your fire is also your "living room" at night, the place where you'll sit around and talk. So make sure you can set up chairs or wood stumps for the gathering.

SUPPLIES

Your fire location in a campsite should be relatively close to your fuel supply, whenever possible. Part of planning a campsite is finding a location where there are sufficient natural materials for building a shelter and to keep your fire going.

But sometimes legal or other considerations require you to build your fire and campsite some distance from the source of your firewood. In those cases, you'll just have to use your creative ingenuity to carry, drag, or roll your firewood to your campsite.

VISIBILITY

Next, do you want to be seen? If so, your fire should be built on a high area, free of obstructions. And if you should be lost, you can make your fire smokey by adding green brush, or punky wood.

But, maybe you *don't* want to be seen. Maybe you're being pursued, or you just want to be left alone—but you need the benefits of a fire. A fire can be built in a deep hole, so that no one can see it except maybe from an airplane. Such a fire should be kept small, and you should add no punky wood to it, otherwise you'll get a lot of smoke.

A fire needn't be huge in order to provide warmth and cooking fuel. I have seen small fires built in ravines where the campers did not want to be noticed. A small fire requires minimal fuel, and is easy to extinguish.

WHAT IS NEEDED TO CREATE A FIRE?

The three essentials for fire are taught to every Scout and camper: heat, fuel, oxygen. Those three are sometimes referred to as the Fire Triangle, the three keys to creating a fire.

Remove any one of these, and you do not have fire! It's pretty self-evident.

HEAT

The heat can come from nature, such as a lightning strike, or the sun shining through a lens, or even the flow of lava. It can come from your spinning of your drill onto a piece of wood, creating temperatures of 400 degrees Fahrenheit and more.

OXYGEN

The oxygen is necessary, and if you can remove the oxygen from a fire, the fire is extinguished. Ever seen a little candle burning, and then someone puts a cup over it? The oxygen is used up quickly and the flame goes out. The air that we all breathe contains 21 percent oxygen; there must be at least 16 percent oxygen in the air for the fire to get started and stay maintained. Have you ever watched a camper huffing and puffing on his campfire to get it going, and keep it going? He's giving it oxygen.

FUEL

Fuel is anything that the flame will consume, which includes a broad diversity of materials. In nature, we're usually talking about burning wood products and plant materials. Obviously, some woods burn better than others. You want dead wood, dry wood, and if you want a quick fire, you want materials that are not too dense. There is a LOT of fuel in nature.

QUIZ

1. Is it a good idea to build a little fire in your primitive wilderness shelter?
2. What are the three necessary ingredients for fire?
3. What is the purpose of a "fire lay"?

ANSWERS

1. Of course not. Most brush shelters are all flammable material. Build your fire just outside the entrance, and keep it small. Or, heat rocks and roll them into your shelter.
2. Oxygen, fuel, heat.
3. A carefully constructed fire lay helps assure that your fire will succeed. A tipi shape, for example, brings the heat quickly to a point and assures a fire.

ACTION:

On a rainy day, try to build a fire outdoors.

SMOKE SIGNALS:

"The hand drill was universal and ancient. Mayan hieroglyphs of the fire-making hand drill extend back in an unbroken line to the Olmec iconography of San Lorenzo—the first American Indian civilization—some 3,000 years ago. Undoubtedly the skill is thousands of years older, lost in the Paleolithic."—*Survival Skills of Native California*, Paul Campbell

CHAPTER 3

THE FOUR PRINCIPLES BY WHICH FIRE IS CREATED: CHEMICALS, ELECTRICITY, THE SUN, FRICTION (OR COMBINATION THEREOF)

Let's start with something everyone is familiar with: matches and lighters.

A WINTER STORY

I was leading a hiking class during a winter December day in the mountains of the Angeles National Forest. We had hiked several miles up to the approximately 3,000-foot level, and a heavy snow began to fall. It had already been windy and cold, and older snow was here and there on the ground. Our group of twenty or so had built a fire in a sheltered spot, warmed some soup and tea, and we were all eager to get back down the trail to the city now that the snow began.

As we began walking, a woman and about ten young girls appeared out of the mist, like an apparition. I wondered where they'd come from.

"Do you have any matches?" the woman asked. She explained that it was their second day of a five-day campout with her Girl Scouts, and that she'd used up all her book matches the previous day. "Really?" I said, incredulously. I thought to myself, *you came up here with all these girls in the snow for five days in the winter and all you brought were book matches?* It was hard to contain myself. I mean, it's one thing to just leave home without the things you need, if you're by yourself. But when you're responsible for the welfare of others, you just need to take extra precautions.

I told the woman that I did not carry book matches, and that I didn't have a Bic lighter either. But I'd made our earlier cook fire with the magnesium fire starter that I always carry on my keychain. I figured, *we're on our way out, and these folks are in dire need.* I took the fire starter off my keychain and showed the Girl Scout leader how to use it. I scraped some of the magnesium block into some scrap paper, and then scraped the ferrocerium insert so that a shower of sparks ignited the magnesium. *Presto!* A bright fire. The leader smiled and graciously accepted my fire starter, and I told her to be sure and never leave home in the future without at least two ways—preferably three—to make a fire. She nodded, and she and her little children disappeared back into the fog and snow. I presume they made it out okay in the following days because I didn't read about them in the local newspaper.

Needless to say, on our hike back, my hiking class had a lively discussion about the need to carry a fire starter, and everyone speculated on how well the small Girl Scout group would do in the snow during the next few days.

MATCHES

Always be prepared. When you travel in to the back country, you should carry several methods of getting a fire started. But remember, your matches will run out, or they might get wet. So you need to have a few other methods as well.

The early history of the match goes way back to the Chinese hundreds of years ago, and gradually, some early forms of the match as we know it were developed. Our modern match is the result of various chemical combinations which are bound onto a stick or paper, which, when rubbed onto something akin to fine sandpaper, bursts into a flame. (When you use a match, you are utilizing two of the principles by which fire is made—chemicals and friction.)

Stick matches are preferable to book matches. You can buy them by the box and you can store them in a variety of waterproof containers.

In my early years of backpacking, I always carried stick matches, and I wrapped them in tinfoil and then protected them even further in a tin canister or jar. I knew that I needed fire, and I wanted my matches to work. These were ordinary stick matches that you buy by the box. As long as they were dry, they worked well.

Of course, it wasn't just that match that was important, but also the striking surface. With no suitable striking surface, you can go through many matches before you get a flame. It's a good idea to store a piece of very fine sandpaper with your fire gear so you're sure to get a flame from your matches.

These days, there are numerous wind-proof stick matches available that are well worth the extra few cents that you pay. These have a larger head, maybe an inch and a half long, and after you strike it, it flames for up to ten seconds before it just burns the woods. These are excellent when there is a slight wind to get your fire going.

BOOK MATCHES

Book matches are still very common, and anytime you purchase cigarettes or cigars, the proprietor typically gives you a book of matches. Sometimes these are printed up with a business's name and given out as free advertisements for the company.

To make book matches last longer, I have seen people carefully split them in half so you theoretically have two matches. Some folks are good at this, but if you haven't practiced this method, you may end up with no match rather than two.

If you're going to rely on book matches to get your fires started, be sure to carry many, and be sure to carry them in a waterproof container, such as a Ziploc plastic bag.

Book matches. They're okay, until they are used up or wet.

THE ART OF LIGHTING A MATCH

Like so many things that people used to do without even thinking about it, striking a book match is becoming something that seems to belong to the quaint past.

During a fire-making class attended by mostly children, my assistant, James Ruther, suggested that rather than jumping into the primitive methods of starting a fire, we should teach the children how to strike a match. It seemed all too simple, I thought.

We began by giving the young students a match book, and asking them to light a match. Most managed to tear a match out of the book, but not one managed to strike the match head across the striking surface in such a way to actually get a flame! Needless to say, I was a bit surprised. But before you argue that these were just young students, there were a few adults present who also had trouble striking a book match!

Begin by carefully pulling out a match, then closing the book, and then holding the match between your fingers. Though there are a few ways you can hold the match between the fingers, the most common is between the thumb and index finger. Assuming the person is right-handed, firmly hold the book in the left hand, and evenly strike the match across the surface.

It's not difficult, as long as the matches, or striking surface, are not old.

STICK MATCHES

Stick matches are several notches above book matches. They are more substantial, they don't fall apart with a little moisture, and there's a bit more to burn. You should choose these over book matches, and carry them in secure waterproof containers.

Camping stores sell stick matches with the longer heads. These are definitely worth the 50 cents to a dollar more you might pay over regular matches. These bigger-headed matches will burn many seconds longer, and will help to assure that you get a fire even in windy or moist conditions.

Stick matches are a notch above book matches. Carry them in a waterproof container. Even better, buy the stick matches with the longer heads.

SHOULD YOU DIP MATCHES IN WAX?

Many articles in backpacking, survival, and hunting magazines have suggested that you can dip your matches in wax to help waterproof and protect them.

In one true story published years ago in the *American Hunter*, a man described how he prepared for a hunting trip. He carefully dipped a hundred or so stick matches into wax, let them dry, and then proudly carried them with him into the woods. When he went to light one of these matches, he reported the disappointment he felt when the first match fizzled but did not light. The second match also fizzled but did not light. The third match fizzled, and so did the entire rest of the box.

The writer pointed out that he did not test his matches before going into the field. Because there are many wax products available, such as beeswax, and various waxes at craft shops, and paraffin (an artificial product), he wasn't making any recommendations, per se, *except* to encourage hikers and campers to test first before they set out. In this man's case, though he had no backup, his fellow hunters fortunately had other methods for fire-starting, so they were able to make a campfire for warmth and cooking.

BUTANE

Carry a butane lighter. In fact, carry as many as you can. Each one is good for a few hundred lights, and they're pretty reliable, unless you step on one.

Al Cornell suggests that you only buy the butane lighters that you can see through, so you know how much fuel you have left.

Yes, they run out of fuel eventually, but even then they are not useless.

During one of our survival skills classes, I found an old discarded Bic lighter with no fuel left. We kept it to demonstrate how you could still get a fire with the use of the sparking wheel. We placed ideal tinder in front of the spark, and we were able to ignite it and get a flame. We experimented with real cotton balls, shredded cedar bark, shredded elder bark, and mugwort, and got flames.

A butane lighter with a see-through body lets you know when you're out of fuel.

A standard butane lighter.

A cigarette lighter that you can refill indefinitely.

ATOMIC LIGHTER

Besides the standards, you can also buy an "atomic lighter," which *appears* to be an ordinary refillable butane lighter, but it's not. Rather than refill with any fuel, you plug it into a USB port and charge a battery. Then, when you light it, two ports produce an electric flame good enough to light your cigar or tinder. It's very high tech, and you need an electrical outlet to recharge it occasionally. If you're very ingenious, you get a little solar panel and recharge this lighter with the sun!

MAKING FIRE WITH THE SUN

The sun is your friend and if you can focus the sun's rays to a point, you can make a fire.

For making a fire, you are either focusing the light through a lens, as with a magnifying glass, or you are focusing the light out and away from the reflector, as with a parabolic dish.

Let's look at each of these.

Shining Light through a Lens

MAGNIFYING GLASS

Perhaps the easiest method for making a fire with the sun is to have a little magnifying glass in your pack or purse. The key to creating a fire with one of these is to have ideal tinder, and to then coax your little embers into a flame. Hold your magnifying glass steady and perpendicular to the rays of the sun so that you get a fine point of light. Hold that fine point of light on the tinder and you should start to see smoke within seconds. As the tiny ember grows, you can blow on it, but gently. As the ember gets bigger, you can blow even harder, and eventually your tinder will burst into flame.

The magnifying glass will focus the sun's rays to a point. With ideal tinder, this is a good way to create a fire. Drawing by the author.

FRESNEL LENS

The Fresnel lens (pronounced "fresh-nel") is typically made of plastic, and can be a powerful way to get a fire with the sun. It can be about 8 by 10 inches (or larger), or it can be the size of a credit card which fits into your wallet. The bigger

The Fresnel lens works like a magnifying glass to focus the rays of the sun to a point. Alan Halcon demonstrates how to use the Fresnel lens.

it is, the better, because it captures and focuses more light. In classrooms of the past, every overhead projector had a Fresnel lens on its top flat surface.

This lens consists of concentric rings etched into the plastic, so that it actually functions like a parabolic dish. They are used to make simple Boy Scout solar cookers, for etching in wood with the sun, and for camera obscuras. They make excellent fire starters.

Small Fresnel lenses are readily available at stationery stores, and larger ones are often available at discount stores. Buy all you can find, as these make excellent gifts to friends and family.

To be safe, wear sun glasses when you try this method because the focal point of light is very bright.

PIGGY'S SPECS

Do you remember *Lord of the Flies*? The plane crashes, all the adults die, and all these young boys go wild and develop two diverse camps. It's a good story with lots of current social commentary.

The boys on the island made fire with Piggy's specs—his reading glasses. You can make a fire with most reading glasses, whether plastic or glass, because they are simply magnifiers.

Not all prescription glasses can be used to make a fire, however. Depending on the eye condition that the glasses were made to correct, they may or may not be able to sufficiently focus the sun's rays to a point. You just have to try it and see if they work.

The key is to use good tinder and hold the glasses steady as you find the focal point. Make sure the glasses are perpendicular to the sun so that the light shines directly through the lens. You'll see right away whether or not this will work. If it works, on a sunny day you'll get a fine point of light and your tinder will start smoking pretty quickly.

CAMERA LENS

Back in the ancient days of 35mm cameras, you could screw off the lens and use it as a magnifier to make a fire. Even if the lens did not come off, you could usually open the back of the camera, where you put in the film, and let the light shine through the camera and through the lens to make your fire.

Though you're not likely to have one of those old cameras anymore, there are still detachable lenses built for digital cameras, and these are still useful as fire starters.

USING ICE

The only natural way to create fire with the sun is to create a lens from a clear sheet of ice. Inuit people did this in the old days with a huge sheet of ice, about four feet in diameter, and carefully scraped to make a lens. Success with this method requires a clear piece of ice, which you can then carefully scrape to create enough of a lens which will focus light onto your tinder. The user would stand the piece of ice vertically, with the flat surface facing the sun, so that the sun's rays would ignite the dry tinder.

Good to know, but there is a simpler way to make fire using water . . .

WATER IN A PLASTIC BOTTLE

Get a clear plastic water container and put just a little water in the bottom. You then hold it up to the sun, and you need to tilt it just-so, so the sun shines through the water like a lens. If you can get a good focal point, hold some tinder at the focal point and if everything is just-so, meaning the sky is clear and the water container is clear and not opaque, then you can get a little ember within minutes.

Primitive fire teacher Gary Gonzales of Palmdale, California, has demonstrated this tactic, and has produced an ember in under two minutes. Success for this method requires a clear plastic container, preferably without ridges in the plastic, and the great patience of Gary.

RIFLE SCOPE

Rifle scopes are also a way to start a fire, using the scope as a magnifying glass. If you have a rifle scope, you should go into your backyard and see if it will work for a fire starter. Again, depending on the size, you're likely to have mixed results.

Focusing the Light Back Away from the Lens

THE ALUMINUM CAN

You can actually make a fire using the bottom of an aluminum beer or soda can, if all the conditions are right. The very bottom of most aluminum cans (beer or cola) is not a true parabolic dish; however, when highly polished, it can be used to focus the sun's rays to a point and ignite tinder.

Since aluminum cans are discarded everywhere, this is valuable information. The fact that we can make a fire from the aluminum can makes this piece of "trash" extremely valuable.

POLISHING THE BOTTOM

You need to give the bottom of the can a high polish in order for it to sufficiently focus the sun's rays. This is easiest done with some fine steel wool. You will need to polish the bottom for about fifteen to twenty minutes, until you have an obviously bright and highly reflective surface. How do you know you are done? You test it, and see how well you can make a fire.

Some folks have suggested that this polishing be done with chocolate. I have tried this and found it unsatisfactory. Chocolate doesn't polish as well as steel wool, and seems to take at least twice as long to get the polish of steel wool. So why is chocolate recommended? I assume it is because a hiker or camper is likely to have chocolate in their pack, which could be the best polishing agent available under those circumstances. Toothpaste seems to also work as a polishing agent, but fine steel wool is my first choice.

Polishing the concave bottom of an aluminum cola can with some fine steel wool.

DOING IT

Point the bottom of the can toward the sun, and then move your tinder into the bottom area, watching for the place where the light focuses to a point. When you find that point, keep your tinder there until you get your coal. This is akin to making a fire with a magnifying glass, except you are not focusing the light through the lens, but back up to a single point.

You may see that there is not a single fine point of light, such as you get with a magnifying glass. Rather, it is a smallish area where the light is focused. You will want to keep your can and tinder stabilized in one point for this to work. You'll find that it's best to put the can on the ground and carefully hold it in one place, with the bottom aimed at the sun.

Fire researcher Eric Zammit found that he could fairly easily ignite rolled mugwort leaves using this method, as long as the bottom of the can was highly polished, and as long as it was close to midday when the sun was directly overhead. He could not ignite paper, though he was able to ignite leaves. Zammit had the best results by holding the can in his hands, and propping his elbows on his

The bottom of the can must be pointed directly at the sun, and the tinder must be held steadily in the focal point of light.

Smoke begins to arise from the tinder.

knees. Then he aligned the can with the sun by watching the can's shadow until the shadow corresponded with the diameter of the can.

"By holding the can at eye level, I could look under the mugwort to find the focal point of the light, and to put it right on the tip of the mugwort," says Zammit.

USING A SOLAR COOKER TO MAKE A FIRE

During my wild food cooking classes, we've cooked some excellent meals with the OneSource solar cooker, which is a parabolic dish cooker which focuses sunlight to a broad point. It can also double as a fire starter. This is not something you'd carry in your pack or pocket, since it's about four feet across, but you might have one in your backyard or in your car. This is a serious solar cooker, based around the parabolic dish which focuses the sunlight to an area that does the cooking. This is the cooker to have in your backyard for emergency cooking, or when the kitchen is too hot in the summer.

The focal point of this cooker gets very hot—at least 400 degrees Fahrenheit. We have found that a piece of paper held in the focal point will burn within twenty seconds!

Placing a piece of paper at the focal point of the solar cooker, just under the frying pan.

The paper is reaching a combustible temperature.

This paper burst into flame in about forty seconds.

A PARABOLIC DISH FIRE STARTER IN YOUR CAR

Your headlamp reflector is a parabolic dish, or at least is reflective enough to make a fire. Your first job is to remove your headlamp. Depending on the make

Piero del Valle and a student steadily hold some tinder in the focal point of this headlamp reflector, which is pointed at the sun.

and model of your car, this can be as easy as removing four screws, or it could be a bit more complicated.

Once you've removed the headlamp, pull it free from the electrical connection. Next, carefully break the glass. Yes, this means that you won't be putting that headlamp back onto the car, so think carefully before you do this with the car you're driving. Also, since this requires the sun, do not ruin your headlamp if the sky is overcast.

Once you break away the glass and clean the edges, you'll see that the inside is a more or less parabolic reflector. On some vehicles, this reflector is round (such as on most Jeeps), and on some cars it's somewhat rectangular.

Face the reflector at the sun, and stick your finger about an inch or so away from the middle of the reflector. You should quickly find the "hot spot." Now get some of that ideal tinder you've been collecting and hold it steady in that hot spot.

Depending on the configuration of the reflector, and on any obstructions to the sun (clouds, haze, trees), you could get a quick ember and flame in less than a minute, or it might take considerably longer. But if everything is just right, this is a remarkably effective way to get a fire going. If you want to know if your headlamp reflector would actually work to make a fire in an emergency, I suggest you go to an auto supply store and buy a headlamp for your car. Then just test it and you'll know.

We don't recommend this method unless you have absolutely no other way to get that fire going.

STAINLESS STEEL SALAD BOWL

Outdoor educator Alan Halcon shared a fascinating experience with me. Alan is an expert in making fire the primitive ways, and he often teaches classes on this subject. During one of his jobs, he was outside where there were tables with food set up for a party. No one was at the tables yet, but Alan noticed from a distance that smoke was coming from one of the bowls. He went over and saw that potato chips in a large stainless steel bowl were smoking. Many were blackened, and so Alan put out the smouldering fire.

He examined what had happened, and realized that the new stainless steel bowl was acting as a parabolic dish, focusing the light to a point. It wasn't a true parabola with a sharp focal point, but since the sun was directly overhead, it was enough focused sunlight to ignite the ideal tinder—greasy potato chips!

Later, Alan purchased a similar large stainless steel bowl and used it in his classes to demonstrate yet another way in which fire can be produced from the sun.

MAKING FIRE WITH FRICTION

Here is the time-proven method of the ages, how ancient people made fire. Each has its pros and cons, and we'll explore them all. We will compare and contrast each in a chart.

THE PLOW

In the movie *Castaway*, we watched as the stranded Tom Hanks figured out how to get a fire using a method known as the plow. Is that a practical way to get a fire?

The plow consists of a long drill—ideally about two feet long, and perhaps three times as thick as a pencil. The base piece, or hearth, is a larger piece of dry wood, ideally at least a half foot wide and maybe two feet long. You secure the hearth with your foot, and then you lean into it with the drill, rubbing it back and forth onto the hearth, which quickly creates a groove. Your rubbing plow will tend to stay in this groove, and smoke will quickly appear from the sides and the very tip of the groove. You'll work hard, and probably feel like you just ran a mile, and maybe, just maybe, that dust at the tip of the groove will develop into a red-hot ember which you can then put into tinder and blow into a flame.

Former Marine Geoff Angle reported that he observed the plow being used to make fire during one of his visits to a Polynesian cultural center. He said he even watched children get an ember. Geoff gave it a try, and he said, "I was sweating like a work horse, and didn't get an ember!" The fact that some children could do this with apparent ease is probably a result of having practiced it for

Making fire with the fire plow in old Hawaii.

Gary Gonzales demonstrates the principle of the fire plow to students. He rubs the drill back and forth onto the hearth longitudinally.

years, using the ideal tinder (dried palm wood), and having just the right finesse and touch to create the ember.

Yes, it can be done, but I feel that other methods are more promising, and more likely to yield the desired results in much less time for the beginning students aspiring to master the art of fire.

In the book *Ancient Hawai'i* by Herb Kawainui Kane, the author paints a picture of what Hawaii might have looked like to early foreign visitors, such as Captain Cook's expedition in the late 1700s. He describes the types of houses you might see, and the fire-making that would have occurred in the smaller houses where more mundane tasks would be performed. "You may see a man or boy making fire by the plow method, vigorously rubbing the end of a hardwood stick along a groove in a block of soft wood until friction ignites the wood dust accumulating at the end of the groove. A metaphor for sexual union, the work of making fire is restricted to men. Smoke or wisps of steam issuing from under crude shelters betray the presence of the family's earth ovens (imu) . . . "

BAMBOO FIRE SAW: Part One

There are several variations of the bamboo fire saw. Here is one.

Begin with a piece of bamboo nearly three inches in diameter, and approximately three feet long. This piece is split in half, longitudinally. This piece is laid on the ground, staked in place so that one edge points up. It takes about

Al Cornell arranges his pieces of split bamboo in preparation for a bamboo fire-making demonstration.

four stakes to secure. Then, the other piece of bamboo is prepared. This second piece will be placed perpendicular to the first piece, with the rounded part of the upper bamboo piece facing down. At the point of contact, a slight groove is

With the lower piece of split bamboo set vertically, Cornell places another split bamboo across it, with the open end up. A small notch is cut into the bottom of the upper piece, where the tinder will be placed.

While Cornell holds the lower piece vertically, his student quickly rubs the cross piece back and forth, holding the tinder in place at the cross point.

cut into the upper piece of bamboo so that it could slide easily on the top of the lower piece.

At that point of contact, place some tinder (probably mugwort) and cover it with a piece of leather. Then, kneel in front of the bamboo, securing the lower piece of bamboo between your knees. Your partner needs to hold onto the lower piece (with a rag or gloves) to make sure it stays vertical. Then work away. You lean into this, rubbing the horizontal upper piece onto the lower piece of bamboo back and forth, trying to cover as much territory as possible, and trying to bear down as hard as you can.

All of this tends to cause the lower piece of bamboo to lay down horizontally, so it's no small task keeping the lower piece of bamboo vertical. While doing this rubbing, you're also holding the leather in place, which holds the mugwort in place, which is right on top of the point-of-contact groove so the heat will ignite the mugwort. Back and forth, and back and forth.

Keep it up and you'll get your ember. You then carefully remove the leather, pick out the ember, put it into some tinder, and puff it into a flame.

Though this would not be my fire-starting method of choice, I have done it several times in the years that followed. I've found it to be a reliable way to get an ember, and particularly good for its unifying effect of people working together.

BAMBOO FIRE SAW: Part Two

There's another method of making fire with bamboo which is practiced in Hawaii and other Pacific islands.

First, split a long section of bamboo longitudinally down the middle, so it is maybe two feet long. Set the half on the ground, rounded side up. Cut a slight slit into the top of the bamboo half. Then, cut a saw-shaped piece of bamboo about a foot and a half long. This saw needs to be cut in such a way that it is as flat as possible. The bottom edge of the saw, the cutting edge, is then sharpened so that it fits well into the slit just cut on the half-round section of bamboo.

Place tinder under the slit, and put your left foot on the half-round section of bamboo to secure it. Then, holding the bamboo saw in your right hand, begin sawing motions in the slit, and continue this way, gradually increasing

Monica Montoya is getting ready to demonstrate one method of making fire with bamboo. While securing a split piece of bamboo on the ground with her knee, she will rub the other piece of split bamboo back and forth, perpendicular to the lower piece of bamboo. The ember is formed underneath the bottom piece of bamboo.

the pressure. Dust develops in the tinder under the slit, and eventually, a small ember is produced. As with all other friction methods, then carefully put the small ember into some good tinder, and slowly and carefully blow it into a flame.

FIRE PISTON

There are many variations of the fire piston. They all have a handle connected to a long dowel, and the dowel fits perfectly into a long hole on a second piece. This tool must be carefully machined to get a good fit.

The very tip of the dowel is hollowed out, so you can insert some tinder into it. The dowel should be oiled and kept clean so it slides easily into the hole. The dowel even has a ring on it—comparable to the rings on your car's pistons—to trap the air when you whack the dowel into the hole.

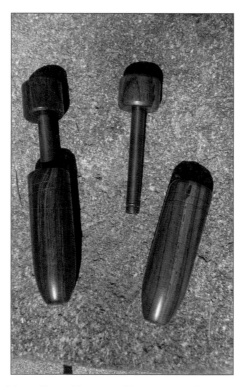

A view of two fire pistons. The rod is rammed into the hole of the second piece. Tinder, such as charcloth, is placed into the little hollow at the tip of the rod. If done just so, with the right amount of force, the tinder ignites from the compression of oxygen.

To operate, you put a little bit of charcloth (or other suitable tinder) into the tip of the dowel, and place the dowel into the hole. Holding the dowel in your right hand, place the tip carefully into the hole. Then, holding the tool with your left hand, quickly smack the dowel into the hole. Then, rapidly pull out the dowel, and if it all went well, you'll have an ember in the charcloth that's in the hollow of the dowel.

For this to work well, the dowel must be kept clean and oiled. As the o-ring wears down, you need to replace it. I have seen some fire pistons which use dental floss instead of a small plastic o-ring. You also need ideal tinder, which is carefully placed in the hollow at the tip of the dowel.

In time, as I used this more often, it became dirty and didn't work quickly, if at all. I had to clean the entire tool, and oil it, and so I learned that it wasn't a good idea to carry this around in the pocket of my pack. I obtained a separate container for my fire piston in order to keep it clean and functioning well. Sometimes, I whacked the tool so many times in my effort to get an ember that the palm of my right hand began to ache. It all seemed so easy and simple in the beginning, but I began to open the pocket where I kept my fire piston less and less often. Though it should work quickly and somewhat effortlessly, it did not do so for me. And since it cannot really be readily fabricated in the woods in an emergency, it's not one of my top choices for making a fire.

PUMP DRILL

The pump drill is a simple drill to which is attached a heavy round flywheel. A horizontal flat piece of wood fits over the drill, and strings are attached to each end of this wood handle, up to the top of the drill. You spin the drill to get it going, and then you just let the flywheel keep turning, as you press down to keep the drilling going.

If you're using this to drill holes in shells—one of the most common uses of the pump drill—you'll outfit the tip of the drill with a nail or stone tip. This works really well, and is a great low-technology method for drilling holes. But making a fire with the pump drill is quite another matter.

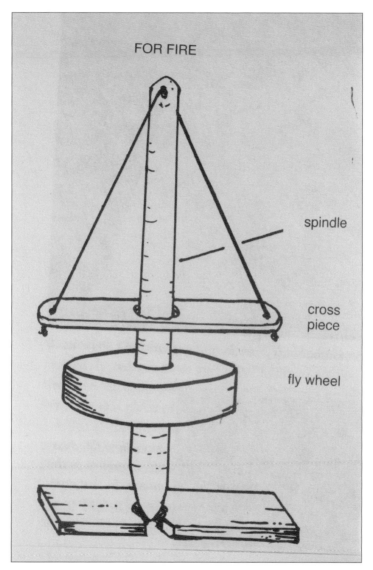

In order to get a fire with a pump drill, you need a large flywheel to keep the drill spinning. Drawing by the author.

Consider: When you're drilling a hole in a shell with a nail point, you're focusing all your pressure to one point, and as the hole gets bigger, the drilling gets easier. However, if you're trying to make a fire, the more you drill, the harder it gets as your pressure points increase. This means that if you are serious about starting a fire this way, you'll need a large and heavy flywheel. If not, you won't be generating the amount of spin that's required to keep the drill spinning, and you won't generate enough heat to get a fire.

Yes, it can be done, but there are better and easier ways to make a fire.

HAND DRILL

The hand drill is the epitome of simplicity. Anthropologist Paul Campbell, author of *Survival Skills of Native California*, believes that this was the most common method used by the most people over most of recorded history. The simple hand drill!

Here are the step-by-step details for success.

You need two pieces: the drill and an approximately eighteen-inch piece of wood about the size of a pencil. I like mulefat for my drills, but many woods will work. Then you also need a hearth, a piece of wood about a foot long, maybe three inches wide, and no more than a half-inch thick. I prefer willow and cottonwood for my hearths, but lots of woods will do the job.

You begin by making a little gouge along one end of the hearth, just back from the edge a half-inch or so. You take the drill, and twirl it with your hands to make that little gouge a bit bigger, big enough so the drill doesn't pop out when you get serious. Then you cut a small triangular notch from the edge of the hearth, to the middle of the gouge, so that the tip of the triangle is in the middle of the gouge. This allows the dust that your drilling produces to flow outward, and allows the heat to create an ember.

There are many ways to do the job, but for a right-handed person, you begin by putting your left foot securely onto the hearth, and kneeling on your right foot. Holding the drill between your hands, you begin spinning at the top of the drill, pressing down firmly as you spin. Your hands will go downward naturally, and when they get too low, you quickly move them up and continue drilling

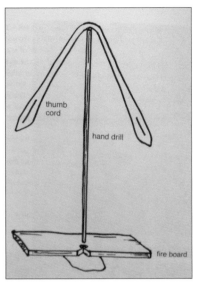

A view of the simplicity of the hand drill, requiring only two pieces of wood. Drawing by the author.

Alan Halcon shows the two pieces of wood required to create an ember with the hand drill. He's holding a willow hearth and a mulefat drill.

from the top. That's how it's done. It will take some time to develop the stamina for this, so expect to practice for a bit without success, as your body and mind figure it all out.

THE THUMB CORD

A way to increase your chances of success with the hand drill involve cutting a thin nock on the top of the drill. Then make a piece of cord with two loops at each end. The total length should be about six inches. Put each thumb into each loop, and loop the cord over the nock in the top of the drill. Now, when you start to drill, you are forced to keep both hands in one position, so you don't have to stop in order to move your hands back up to the top. But it also means you don't get that momentary rest.

You could also have two or more people gathered around the drill, each taking a turn drilling so that no one person does all the work.

Researcher Alan Halcon also made a useful discovery in the mastery of the hand drill. He observed the way different people sat or kneeled when they drilled to make fire. Those that sat back comfortably did not utilize their full potential, because their hands and arms did all the work. Halcon found that the best position was to kneel into the drill, with the body bearing down upon the drill as

Piero del Valle spins the hand drill with the help of the thumb cord.

Jim Robertson demonstrates the use of the hand drill with the assistance of the thumb cord.

Two people working in tandem with the hand drill. As one person's hands move downward on the drill, the next person begins to drill from the top. They continue this way until an ember is created.

one does the work. This provided the greatest pounds of pressure possible, and resulted in quicker and more consistent production of a coal.

While one person keeps their foot on the hearth, three (or more) people can spin the hand drill, one after the other, so that no one person gets too exhausted.

Alan Halcon in a patch of mulefat, looking for ideal hand drills.

Willow hearths and mulefat drills prepared for students.

A COMPARISON OF HAND-DRILL POSTURES

POSITION	DESCRIPTION	POUNDS of PRESSURE
Seated or Cross-legged	The seated position comes in a couple of variations, either crossed leg or one leg slightly extended to hold down the hearth. In either case, your body weight is centered over your rump, which is in contact with the ground. In this position, you are completely dependent on your arms to apply sufficient downward pressure to achieve a coal. For some, this is viable, but for most, this can be very difficult.	19
Prayer or Kneeling Position	As with the seated position, your body weight is centered over the ground under your rump. And, as with the seated position, you rely solely on your arms to apply sufficient downward pressure.	20
Bow-Drill Position	In what I call the bow-drill position, you raise up off your rump and shift your weight forward and nearer over the top of the drill. However, in this position, your arms are still extended. As a result, the ability to apply downward pressure is still reliant only on your arms.	23
The Short-Stance Position	By closing your stance and keeping your elbows bent (instead of outstretching your arms), you can shift more of your weight over the drill, effectively allowing you to apply more downward pressure.	31

Halcon conducted experiments to see how body positions affected the pounds of downward pressure. With the aid of a standard bathroom scale and his favorite hand drill at the time, here are his results.

You can see that the short stance allows one to apply more downward pressure than all of the others. This equates to the ability to produce a coal faster than using the other positions. By doing this, you will also be less fatigued.

Halcon demonstrates the "seated" or "cross-legged position."

Halcon demonstrates the "prayer" or "kneeling position."

Halcon demonstrates the "bow-drill position."

Halcon demonstrates the "short-stance position."

WORLD RECORD

As a child, Halcon was always fascinated with the possibility of making fire with the hand drill or bow drill. As an adult, when someone finally taught him how to do it, he became obsessed, and worked on the hand drill in whatever spare time he had. One day, with seven witnesses, Halcon set up his hearth and drill, and got into position. When the timer said "go," Halcon took one forceful and rapid pass of the drill, and created an ember on his hearth in two seconds! He then repeated the feat a second time, which is widely regarded as the world's fastest ember by the hand drill. (Anyway, how much faster could anyone actually get?)

BOW AND DRILL

The bow and drill gives you a technological advance over the hand drill. You need the hearth and drill as with the hand drill, plus a bow, and a bearing block to push down on the drill.

DOING IT

A description of the components for bow and drill:

Bow	Can be flexible or rigid wood. I've seen a buffalo rib used! The general rule is that it should be about the distance of armpit to wrist of the user.
Bow cord	Natural cordage such as yucca or animal hide. Also good is shoe string, paracord, or quickly twined cordage.
Drill	Dry straight wood, no thicker than a thumb, maybe a foot long. Ideal woods are willow, cottonwood, ash, and others.
Bearing block	Should be harder than drill. Can be many materials such as a bone with a hollow, shot glass (be careful), metal electrical socket, stone with hole, wood burl.
Hearth	Can be same material as drill. Generally, about a foot long, a few inches wide. Good woods are willow, cottonwood, cedar, redwood, ash, etc.
Spark catcher	This is a flat piece of leather, leaf, or bark under the notch. When you get the ember, this catcher allows you to carefully pick up the ember and place it into ideal tinder.

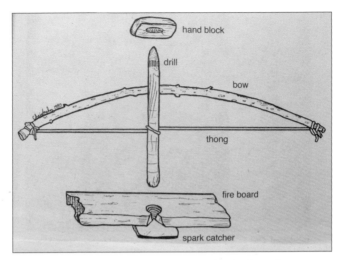

The components of the bow and drill. Drawing by the author.

Body posture is very important when you're trying to make a fire with the bow and drill. Make sure all the parts fit together well. The bottom of the drill should fit into the hole in the hearth. The bearing block should be comfortable in the hand, and the drill should fit into it easily.

Twist the cord around the drill. It should be snug, but not too snug that you cannot move it. And it should not be so loose that it slips when you try to spin it. It needs to be "just right."

Assuming you are right-handed, put your left foot on the hearth, and kneel on your right knee. Twist the cord around the drill, and set it into the hole on the hearth. With your left hand, press the bearing block onto the drill, while locking the inset of your arm around your left knee. Now, slowly begin to spin the drill. Don't go too fast at first, and don't press down too hard. Get the drill moving, keep the drill vertical, and keep the cord more or less in the middle of the drill. Lean into it a bit. Slowly and gradually increase your speed and pressure. If everything was done right, you'll start to see smoke.

Keep it going, and it will smell like burnt coffee. Keep it going as you see the brown dust come into the notch, and eventually, as you continue, there will be black dust. You're almost there. Keep it going, and don't stop yet. Watch that

This man just blew his ember into a flame! On the ground, from the left, see the rock bearing piece, the drill, the bow, the hearth, and the spark catcher.

dust. When you see smoking coming out of the dust pile, you've created your ember. Gently lift the drill out of the hearth, without knocking the hearth about. Your dust should still be smoking. Very gently puff on it. Just a little. You don't want to scatter the dust pile, but rather, you want to gently stoke it so the ember gets bigger, and bigger.

Now, you can carefully pick up the ember on the little piece of leather and place it into your prepared tinder. The ideal prepared tinder for the first phase is dried and shredded yucca, mugwort, elder bark, or cedar bark. There are other materials that could work well too, so just be sure that your tinder holds together, and has enough density so the ember won't just fall through the cracks. Now, holding it up, gently puff into your ember so that it slowly, but surely, gets larger, and grows into the tinder.

Next, add a very large birdnest shape of dried grass or pine needles around that initial bit of tinder, and continue to puff and blow. Smoke will pour out. Sometimes, if there is a breeze, you can just kneel in the dirt and hold your tinder bundle into the wind and let the wind do your work for you. Soon, a flame will burst forth, and you've now joined the ranks of Tom Hanks and the first cavemen who created fire!

Splitting a small log is the first process for making the hearth, which is the basis for the hand drill, or the bow and drill.

Donald shows a blank hearth, just split out from a small log.

Gary Gonzales holds down the hearth while coaching a student at making fire with the bow.

Working on getting a coal with the bow and drill.

Gonzales shows a student how to twist the cord of the bow onto the drill.

Under the tutelage of Gary Gonzales, students start putting all the pieces together for the bow drill.

Student works the bow with right hand. Note that his left hand is locked over his left knee to stabilize his body position. Other students look on.

The author demonstrates making a fire for the students of Stanton Lee. The ember is about to burst into flame. Photo by Helen W. Nyerges.

The author produces a flame with the bow and drill method, for the students of Stanton Lee. Lee is at the right. Photo by Helen W. Nyerges.

TROUBLESHOOTING THE BOW DRILL

PROBLEM	SOLUTION
The bearing block smokes.	You want your friction/pressure on the hearth, so use a harder material for bearing block, or oil the socket.
Bow string breaks.	Work quicker, or get a stronger material.
String slips on drill.	Tighten cord; try carving facets on drill so it's not round.
Too hard to stroke the drill.	Cord is too tight, loosen it.
Drill pops out of hole on hearth.	Make starter hole bigger; make sure hole is set back a bit from edge; keep drill vertical when drilling.
Drill wears through hearth with no ember.	Try again with a new hole. You will need to start increasing pressure and increasing speed. Possibly try different woods.
I get very tired when doing this!!	Yes you do! Have some chia seeds, and try again.

EGYPTIAN BOW-DRILL

We know that the ancient Egyptians used a version of the bow drill because they have been found in tombs.

The main difference between the Egyptian bow-drill and the bow drill described earlier is that the cord of the Egyptian bow-drill is attached to the drill. You can drill a hole through the drill, and tie the cord to it, or you can just tie the cord onto the drill with a few loops.

The advantage of this variation is that your cord does not have to be under the same degree of pressure as is necessary in a regular bow and drill. In fact, I have seen dental floss used as the cord to demonstrate that you can still get an ember with this method with less tension.

Your body posture is more or less the same with the Egyptian bow-drill and the regular bow drill, and the back and forth drilling motion is the same with both. However, with the Egyptian method, you will find that you are holding the bow away from the drill to give the cord the tension that it needs. If you've practiced with the regular bow and drill, this Egyptian method is easy to get used to, and you might even like it more because it does not require the same amount of strength to hold the cord at the appropriate tension. The Egyptian bow-drill set can also be significantly smaller than a regular bow and drill set.

ARCTIC STRAP DRILL

This is essentially another variation of the bow and drill, used by people of the northern Arctic regions and taught to me by Al Cornell, who is one of the biggest proponents of this method. This was a major way to make fire from Siberia all the way around to Greenland and all the way across Central and Upper Canada.

This variation came about in Central Canada, where there was plenty of wood. This method developed about 1000 CE as an adaptation to the bow drill which was easier to carry. This was viewed as a way to make fire by each person alone, when everyone else was gone, or disabled.

All seventeen Inuit groups use this method, as do the Athabascan groups, who, however, carry a small bow instead of the strap. The Inuit pouches were used to carry with drill, board, a few straps, and moss for tinder.

The hearth and drill are essentially the same as a regular bow and drill, but typically much smaller. The bearing block is a small piece of wood that is fitted to the mouth, with a little gouge on the bottom side where the drill will spin. You use a leather thong, which you pull back and forth with your hands to spin the drill.

I've often demonstrated this on a table so everyone could see, because the kit is small and the user is leaning over onto the drill and hearth.

So, set the hearth on solid ground, and get the bearing block secure in your mouth. (You will have to carve it beforehand so it comfortably fits into your mouth.) Secure the hearth with your foot or knee, or have someone else secure it in place. Or, you can do as Cornell does; he kneels on a separate stick, which he calls a "keeper stick," which in turn holds the hearth in place. Put the drill in place, and lean down onto the drill with your mouth, so you're now holding the drill in place with the bearing block. Wrap the leather thong around the drill,

Al Cornell shows the parts of the arctic strap drill. Around his neck is the mouth piece. In his right hand is the small drill. In his left hand is the hearth and cord.

and then carefully pull the thong to the right, to the left, to the right, and keep it up as you get the feel for this. You continue increasing your downward pressure on the drill slightly, and increasing the speed of the drill as you get smoke and eventually your ember.

When you see this done for the first time, you can't help but think that this is a good way to lose an eye, or have a drill go up your nose. But such mishaps are rare, because if the drill pops out of the hearth, it just goes flat on the ground.

Though I can get a fire this way, I am not a big fan of it because it bothers my teeth. But if I had no other choice, this is every bit as viable a method as the regular bow and drill.

Cornell demonstrates the use of the arctic strap drill. With the mouthpiece gripped in his teeth, he presses the drill onto a hearth, while spinning the drill side to side with the leather cord.

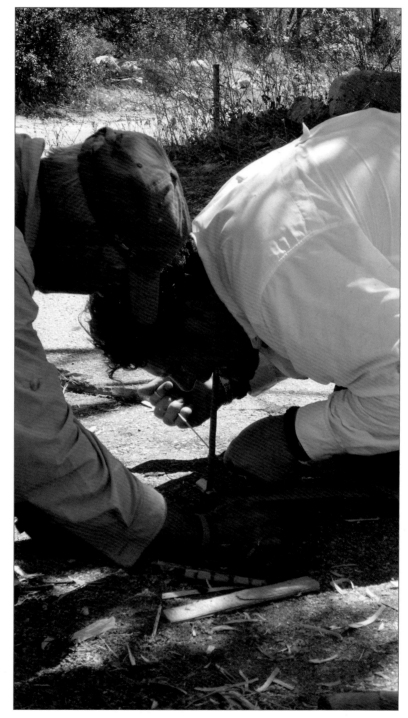

Cornell (left) coaches a student in the use of arctic strap drill.

THE FIRE STRAW

Dude McLean would always carry a straw with him when we were out on the trail. The straw would be used to blow onto an ember deep in an old campfire, and blow it alive by adding new tinder. He also used it when blowing a tinder bundle to a flame, just after the ember was added to the mugwort birdnest. The straw allowed him to blow deep into the tinder, or coals, without having his face right in it. Using a straw for this purpose is as old as the hills, so the only new thing is that Dude McLean had the audacity to tell others that he invented the fire straw. He'd pull out a foot-long piece of elder stem which he'd hollowed out and carved "fire straw" onto its bark. We knew he didn't invent it, but it brought a lot of laughs, and it really was the coolest fire straw anyone had ever seen!

FLINT AND STEEL

This was also one of the most widely practiced method of fire-making throughout the world, second only to the hand drill.

You begin with a piece of flint, or any other sparkable rock. You can experiment to find a sparkable rock, and there are many which will work. This includes chert, petrified wood, quartzite, and others. You can try taking a beach cobble and breaking it. If it reveals a sparkly inside, that means a high quartz content, and it should work well for fire-making.

You also need a piece of carbon steel, that is, rustable steel. My very first steel was from a Girl Scout fire-making kit. It was just a flat piece of an old carbon steel file. You can also purchase bastard files from the hardware store and use them with great success. Also, some blacksmiths make the C-shaped steels used expressly for fire-making.

Then you need some ideal tinder to ignite. Willow or cattail fluff will ignite well with a spark, but most flint and steel practitioners prefer to use something called charcloth for their tinder. (See sidebar on making charcloth.)

A C-shaped carbon steel striker, made by a blacksmith expressly for making fire with flint and steel.

Gonzales instructs a student in the proper way to hold the charcloth under the flint, and how to strike with the steel.

Gonzales ready for action. Note the striker wrapped around right fist, and flint in left hand. A little piece of charcloth is under the flint.

Gonzales is ready to strike downward.

You can see some of the sparks as Gonzales follows through with a sharp glancing blow to the flint.

Andrew Do modified a steel striker so that it can double as a caribeener.

First, practice striking the flint with your steel so you can feel the amount of strength and pressure required to produce a shower of sparks. There are many ways this has been done, but here's a good method for a right-handed person.

Hold the steel striker in your right hand, and hold a flake of flint in your left hand, between thumb and index finger. To produce a shower of sparks, strike down hard onto the flint with the striker, and follow through. It's a sharp, perpendicular strike of edge to edge. You'll get a shower of sparks if you hit it hard enough.

Then, place a bit of charcloth (or other tinder) either directly under the flint or between your next two fingers. Now strike again, and watch the black charcloth. If you produced a good shower of sparks, and if your charcloth was "just so," one of the little sparks will stick on the charcloth. Sometimes you don't see it at first, but a small spot on the charcloth will be glowing red. You've captured a spark.

Now, gently blow onto the charcloth, and watch the ember grow. Quickly place the charcloth into your prepared tinder. Your prepared tinder should ideally be a birdnest shape of dry grass, pine needles, shredded bark—whatever tinder that is available to you, and that you're familiar with using.

Now, after you've placed the glowing charcloth into your tinder bundle, gently blow into the bundle. The ember will grow. Continue doing this as the ember begins to burn the tinder and it will continue to grow larger. Continue to blow. If there is a breeze, that can work to your advantage by turning the tinder to face the wind. Soon, your tinder will eventually burst into flame.

MAKING CHARCLOTH

Planning ahead to made a primitive fire is part of your success formula. You need good dry tinder, and you need it in a container to keep it dry.

Charcloth is not the only available tinder, but it is one that you can make out of any natural fabric. It's most commonly made from old cotton pants or t-shirts. You'll need old cotton, and you'll need a can about the size of a shoe-polish can or an Altoids tin, with a snug-fitting lid.

Cut up pieces of the cotton so they all fit neatly into the can. Punch a nail-sized hole into the lid of the can, and place the lid on securely. Now, place the can into your fire. It should puff out white smoke in a few minutes. This will only take five minutes or so, after which you can knock the can out of the fire and let it cool. When you open the can—assuming you did everything right and everything went well—you will have all black charcloth.

Gary Gonzales shows what charcloth should look like after the can of cotton has been in the fire for a few minutes.

But sometimes it doesn't all go right. If the cotton is obviously only partially charred, then put the lid back on and put in back into the fire for a few more minutes. If you opened up the can and it's all white ash, it means your little hole was too big and you just burned the cotton to ash. Try again.

If you end up with what looks like a little hockey puck, it means you didn't have cotton fabric but polyester which just melted into one piece. Throw it away and start all over with 100 percent cotton.

MARCASITE: Hitting two rocks together

Have you ever heard someone say that they thought you could make fire by striking two rocks together? This is possible, but not with two pieces of flint, or quartzite.

If someone successfully produced enough sparks to make a fire by hitting two rocks, then one of the rocks was marcasite, and the other was any of the "sparkable" (high quartz content) rocks that are used with flint and steel (such as flint, chert, quartzite, etc.).

Marcasite is sometimes called white iron pyrite, or iron sulfide. Geologists describe it as having an orthorhombic crystal structure, distinct from pyrite, or the so-called "fools' gold." Marcasite is a brittle material that cannot be scratched with a knife. The thin, flat, tabular crystals, when joined in groups, are called "cockscombs."

To make fire with marcasite and flint, you are performing the same action as you would with a piece of flint and steel. You hold one steady, and you sharply strike the other. Once your technique is sufficient to produce sparks, you then add charcloth, or any of the other spark-catching materials.

Marcasite, left, and a piece of flint.

Cornell typically puts the marcasite on the ground and whacks it with a piece of flint. Dull sparks are produced; if you go into a dark room, you'll see the sparks more clearly.

According to Al Cornell, this method revolutionized fire-making in the latter Paleolithic era, roughly ending ten thousand or eleven thousand years ago in Europe, since the use of the more tedious hand drill was no longer necessary.

In the Arctic, marcasite would often be carried as a backup to the strap drill circa 1000 CE up to the arrival of steel.

Pieces of marcasite.

MAKING FIRE WITH CHEMISTRY

POTASSIUM PERMANGANATE

Certain chemicals are ideal for creating a fire, with little work. Here is a good example.

Pour about a half cup of potassium permanganate into a metal container. This chemical comes as a black powder. Create a little dimple in the middle of the potassium permanganate, and then pour a little glycerin into the dimple. Then stand back.

After a minute or two—sometimes longer—the mixture starts to smoke, and then suddenly, *poof*! It all goes up in flame, burning hot for a minute or so before it's burned out. It's an excellent way to get a fire started, and it's an excellent way to entertain a bunch of young campers. But to be fair, who carries glycerin and potassium permanganate?

The demonstration of making fire with potassium permanganate and glycerin is a good crowd-pleaser, and it serves to demonstrate the power and destructive potential of fire.

FLARE

Do you carry a flare in your car? It should be a regular, automatic part of your automobile supplies, for signaling to other drivers in a roadside emergency. But flares don't last forever, so you should buy new ones approximately every two years.

Your flare is an excellent fire starter. You peel off the top and scrape the two pieces together to get an ignition. The flare will then burn hotly for fifteen to thirty minutes. If your car won't start and you have to spend the night in the winter woods, use that flare to get your fire going!

FERROCERIUM

These days, every backpacking store and online store has dozens of clever new ways to make a fire. Most are based on the ferrocerium rod, which are black rods about the thickness of a pencil (they vary), and anywhere from a few inches to half a foot long. You scrape it with your knife, and *presto!*, you get a shower of sparks. Some knives even have these built into the handle.

The really pretty ferrocerium rods that you can buy at sports or gun shows are mounted on a piece of antler or wood. These are very effective, and beautiful, though you're paying more than necessary because of the "wow" factor.

MAGNESIUM FIRE STARTER

The magnesium fire starter is manufactured in the United States by the Doan Company of Cleveland, Ohio.

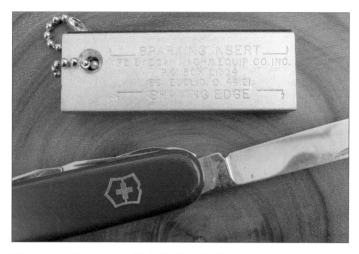

Magnesium fire starter, with Swiss Army knife.

After scraping shavings of magnesium into tinder, you scrape the ferrocerium rod to create sparks and ignite the magnesium.

The spark from the ferrocerium of the magnesium fire-starting tool.

Carlos Hall shows the original magnesium fire starter from the Doan company.

The tool is a little rectangle of a mix of magnesium and other ingredients (kept secret by the manufacturer), and a thin ferrocerium rod secured to the long end of the tool. A hole is drilled into the bar so that it can be carried at all times on one's key chain.

This magnesium fire starter measures about an inch wide, by three inches long, by about a quarter-inch thick. You take your knife and scrape a pile of

Andrew Do modified the original Doan fire starter by cutting it smaller and drilling a little hole, making a smaller fire starter that fits in his pocket.

magnesium onto some tinder, and then you scrape the built-in ferrocerium rod to produce a shower of sparks. Presto! You have a flame. Now you build it up with small tinder and twigs and get your fire going.

I like this tool among all the myriad fire-starter tools currently available at the backpacking shops because there are no moving parts (nothing to break), and nothing to refill (no liquids). It's basic and simple.

I met the inventor of this tool in 1997 at his home in Ohio. Sol Levenson told me that he noted in his metal shop that you had to be meticulously clean when working with magnesium, because the shavings were so flammable. Machine and metal shops that work magnesium have actually burned to the ground when a stray spark flew into magnesium shavings. Fortunately, that never happened with Levenson. He used to look at those shavings and think to himself, *Hmm, this could be a useful camping tool.* The company has made millions of these, and it has even become a standard item in military survival kits.

TROUBLESHOOTING

If you have difficulty with the magnesium fire starter, try this.

First, make sure you get a sufficient pile of shavings. If your knife is dull, or you're not bearing down hard enough, you'll end up with a little pile of small shavings. Try again.

Next, control your knife. Don't scrape the ferrocerium side of the tool too hard, where you bring down your knife too far and scatter all the shavings they've just worked so hard to create.

Lastly, you must do this out of the wind, or the wind will scatter your shavings in all directions. You also need a solid foundation to do this, for if you try to scrape the shavings onto something like pine needles, all the shavings get lost in the needles and they are impossible to collect into a small pile.

KNOCK-OFFS

If you've been to gun shows, knife shows, or survival shows, you've undoubtedly seen various magnesium fire starters inspired by Sol Levenson's invention. And they come in all shapes and sizes. Most consist of a rod of ferrocerium and a rod of magnesium, epoxied together. Some are fastened to bits of wood or antler. Most work well, are great conversation pieces, and are much more expensive than Sol's original simple invention. But some flat-out don't work, especially the Chinese knock-off that costs only a few dollars. If you want a magnesium fire starter that works, buy an original from Doan.

USING A ROUND OF SHOTGUN AMMO

If you're out hunting, and you get lost and need to spend the night in the woods, there is a way to make a fire with your shotgun and some ammo.

You can easily cut open the top of the shotgun round, remove the wadding, and pour the powder into tinder. Then you ignite it with your magnifying glass. But be careful and make sure you put the powder into good tinder, because you *will* get a fire, and it will ignite (and be over) very quickly. You must be ready for success with your ideal tinder.

If it happens to be overcast or nighttime, there's another way to make a fire with your shotgun. Cut open the top of the shotgun round, and remove the wadding. Insert some cotton into the round, such as a piece of cotton you've cut from

Jamie Schultz shows a twelve-gauge shotgun shell.

your handkerchief or clothing. Just make sure it's cotton, not polyester. Try to close the top of the round, if you can. Load the round, and fire it in a safe direction. It won't go very far—it's just cotton after all. But the cotton will come out burning or glowing, and then you should put that into your carefully prepared tinder and make your tinder. Yes, prepare all your tinder before you fire your shotgun, otherwise you'll get a burning piece of cotton.

FIRE BY ELECTRICITY

In today's world, if you carry a battery, you can start a fire! Let's look at many of the ways in which you can tap electricity for the purpose of making your campfire.

MAKING FIRE FROM A CAR BATTERY

Let's say your car breaks down in the woods. You didn't bring any emergency gear because you had dinner plans and you didn't expect to spend the night in the dark pine forest where no one goes at night. And you didn't bring any matches or other fire starters. What now?

There are many ways to make fire with things that are in, or a part of, your car. Start with the easiest method first. First, collect your flammable tinder and prepare your fire ring in a safe place. Next, push in your cigarette lighter. After a few seconds, it pops out and the inside is red hot. Get it out of the car, press some tinder into the hot end, and blow on it gently until you get your flame. Add some tinder and get that fire going.

Okay, so you don't have the cigarette lighter. Now what?

Pop the hood of your vehicle and locate your battery. If you really aren't certain which is the battery, it's that black rectangular object and there's typically two fat wires coming out of it, one of which is usually black, and the other red.

Next, find your jumper cables, which should be considered an essential part of every car's emergency gear. Carefully attach the jumper cables, keeping the two free ends from touching. Your jumper cables are color-coded red (positive) and black (negative), so attach two of the copper clamps to each end of the battery.

Positive and negative copper clamps are attached to a wire, with tinder wrapped around the wire. The free negative clamp is attached to the battery. Then, when the free positive clamp touches the battery, electricity flows through the wire and ignites the tinder.

Although you *could* randomly strike the two free terminals of your jumper cables and get a spark, that's not a safe way to do this.

With one of the free ends of your jumper cables, grasp a paper clip or a small piece of wire with the teeth of that clamp. Wrap that wire with a bit of flammable tinder—such as some cotton, or mugwort, or other dry leaves. Then, carefully touch the remaining free clamp to the wire, and again, the tinder ignites as electricity flows through the wire.

Be ready to add that little flame to your prepared pile of tinder and make your fire. Be very careful to then secure the jumper cables so the two free ends do not touch (which could cause a spark, and even explode your battery), and quickly remove the jumper cables from your battery. It really helps to have at least two people working on this.

NO JUMPER CABLES?

Oh, no! You didn't have a jumper cable in your car? That's too bad, but all is not lost. You should still be able to coax a fire from your car battery, though it might be a bit harder.

The key is to make a bridge from the positive to the negative terminal of the battery. One of the ideal ways to do this is with a piece of fine steel wool. Assuming you have some steel wool in your car, you take a piece about a foot long or longer. Touch one end to one battery terminal, touch the other end of the steel wool to the other terminal, and watch out! The steel wool will quickly start to burn. Get it out of the engine compartment and add some tinder and blow it to a flame, adding other tinders.

Since it's more likely that you *don't* have steel wool handy in your car, there are some other options. You should be able to find a short piece of fine wire, somewhere. No thicker than a paper clip, but it has to be long enough to reach from terminal to terminal of the battery. If you have to cannibalize your car for the wire, try to select a wire that is non-critical—perhaps from the radio.

Stretch the wire from terminal to terminal and it should start to get hot. Be ready to wrap some dry cotton or other fibrous material around the wire, and hopefully you'll get that cotton burning in a short while.

MAKING A FIRE FROM FLASHLIGHT BATTERIES

Batteries of the D, C, AA, AAA, and nine-volt can all be used to make a fire, though the nine-volt is the easiest because it has the most voltage.

The easiest way to produce a fire from the nine-volt battery is to simply press the terminals of the nine-volt battery onto some fine steel wool, and *presto!*—the steel wool begins to burn. It's a bit too easy!

With the other batteries, you need to stretch the steel wool from the top terminal to the bottom terminal. Don't just press the steel wool onto a terminal and hold it there, but rather, touch it lightly and move it about until you see the spark begin.

The AA and AAA will be the hardest batteries for fire-making, because they hold the lowest charge. You might need to stack two of them, and have a lot of patience.

Using two D batteries, a piece of fine steel wool is stretched from pole to pole.

D and C cell batteries are fairly easy to use to create a fire. Again, stretch the steel wool from pole to pole, touch it gently and move it about, and you'll see the steel wool begin to spark a bit and then burn. If your batteries are not at full charge, you can try stacking at least two of them, and trying again.

The steel wool has started to burn.

OTHER BATTERIES

These days, most people carry batteries in cell phones, cameras, and other portable devices. The batteries of a cell phone, for example, are flat square batteries that
are relatively easy to remove from the phone. When you look at the terminals,

you'll see three contact points. The easiest way to create a fire from this battery is with the finest steel wool. Simply press the steel wool onto the terminals, and in a few seconds the steel wool will be glowing and burning.

THE VALUE OF STEEL WOOL (and possible alternatives)

The finest steel wool is a virtual life-saver when it comes to making a fire. If you don't have steel wool, there really is no good substitute for it! Possibly you can do some serious McGyver improvising with aluminum foil, aluminum gum wrappers, or fine wire—maybe. It always works really well on television, but not that well in real life. Perhaps you should just try another method for making that fire.

For getting a fire from an electrical source, or for catching that spark from your flint and steel, fine steel wool is the ideal material. Buy a few bags at your local hardware store, and store some in your garage, and some in the trunk of your car.

Here is an overview of the many ways you can make a fire without matches.

The rating is both objective (tests by the author) and subjective (there are many variables hard to quantify). Rating is based upon the ease of an amateur to get a fire consistently, 10 being the easiest method where you will most consistently get success. If any details are unclear, read the text, or consult the listed references. P.S. Yes, there are many other ways to start a fire besides what is listed here.

METHOD	COMMENTS	RATING
	FRICTION	
Bamboo	Rubbing a dry piece of a half-bamboo perpendicular to another.	6.3
Plow	Rubbing a piece of wood onto another flat piece. Everything must be "just so."	4.5
Piston	Must be a well-machined tool; not something you'd make in the wilderness.	4

Pump	Can be done, but there are too many easier methods.	2
Hand drill	With practice, and correct materials, this can be a good standby; thumb-cord seriously improves ability to get ember.	7.8
Bow and drill	A good wilderness standard; the bow gives you a technological advantage over the hand drill.	8.5
Flint and steel	With the right materials, and minimal practice, you can get a flame.	9.2
SUN		
Magnifying glass	Need good tinder and sun.	9
Fresnel lens	This is a specialized magnifying glass, and an awesome fire starter.	9.5
Camera lens	"Old-fashioned" 35mm camera lens were excellent for this; might have to tweak a bit with modern cameras.	7
Eye glasses, reading	Smallish lens, but very effective with good tinder.	8
Bottom of can	Must polish the bottom, takes time and patience.	4
Salad bowl, stainless steel	Get a larger bowl. Works well under right conditions.	6.8
Reflector of headlamp of car	Must break glass from headlamp, but does work well.	7.5
Solar oven, dish-style	Paper will quickly burst into flame when placed into the focal point of a parabolic cooker, on a sunny day.	9
ELECTRICITY		
Car battery	With jumper cables, or steel wool, this produces a sure fire.	7.9
Flashlight battery (C/D)	Need fine steel wool, and maybe at least two batteries.	6
Nine-volt battery	With steel wool, a quick flame.	8.5

Cell phone battery	Need fine steel wool.	6.5
Cigarette lighter in car	Need fine steel wool, or other good flammable tinder.	7
	CHEMICALS	
Potassium permanganate	Need to add glycerin. Works well, but who carries this?	8
Magnesium fire starter	Need a knife. Don't get the inferior knock-offs.	9
A flare	As long as this isn't too old, it's a sure fire.	9.5
Shotgun shell	Read text for the two ways to get a fire from shotgun shell.	7

QUIZ

1. What are the Four Principles by which fire is created?
2. Name at least two ways to make a fire with something that is in your car, or a part of your car.
3. Name two ways to make fire from the sun.
4. Name at least one way to make fire from water.
5. Describe how to make a fire with a discarded beer or cola can.
6. According to research by Alan Halcon, your body position has no bearing on your ability to get an ember with the hand drill. True or False.

ANSWERS

1. The sun, electricity, friction, chemicals.
2. The battery, cigarette lighter, flare, headlamp reflector.
3. Magnifying glass, reading glasses, Fresnel lens, parabolic solar cooker, bottom of a cola can.
4. Shine the sun through water in a clear plastic or glass container. Inuit (in the past) created a lens from clear ice, and created fire by shining the sun through it.
5. Polish the bottom, point it at the sun, put tinder in the hot spot.
6. False.

ACTION:

Make a fire from reading glasses.

Make a fire with steel wool and batteries.

SMOKE SIGNALS:

"The ability to make a fire in the wild is perhaps the most important survival skill one can possess—literally the difference between a dark shivering death and a hot meal in the glow of a warming blaze. It cannot be taught by theory. Only through familiarity with the range of materials and techniques the Indians actually used in a variety of environments and by practice does the fire come forth."—*Survival Skills of Native California*, Paul Campbell

CHAPTER 4

FROM EMBER TO FLAMES: MOTHERING YOUR FIRE

So you've gotten your initial ember or flame started. Now you need to take it through the next few steps, so that you have the campfire that you need.

If you started with a friction method, you've created an ember. Now you must take that ember to flame.

If you started your work with chemicals, electricity, or the sun, you probably have a flame right away. Now you need to nurture it so it grows.

TAKING YOUR EMBER TO A FLAME

Just like a newly born baby, your baby ember needs to be protected! You want your baby to survive childhood, grow up, and become a fully mature "adult" fire.

Stage one:

Begin with the finest fluffy tinder: mugwort, shredded elder bark, cattail, cotton balls, dryer lint. There are many options here, but this first stage must be very fine, and must be able to hold together well.

Keeping the initial ember alive in a bundle of dried mugwort.

Shape your fluffy tinder into a birdnest shape, which will be a bed for your ember. Your birdnest bundle needs to have a combination of light airiness, but it cannot have so many air pockets that you simply lose your ember as it breaks into smaller pieces. This is why a bundle of pine needles doesn't usually work initially. You want materials that hold together well, and allows your ember to grow, and grow.

Alan Halcon shows a cigar of burning mugwort, right. He also holds some of the fresh mugwort leaves.

Carefully place your ember into your fluffy tinder bundle and then gently blow on it. You don't want to blow hard on it, because this can just scatter the ember into tiny pieces which will self-extinguish. Begin gently puffing, and increase the strength when you see that the ember is growing.

REALITY CHECK

When you really, really need that fire, you *must* find something, anything that will allow your little flame or ember to grow. Lint in the bottom of your pockets might work, and so might a paper wrapper to a sandwich or other food. If everything is wet, you can split a dried branch, and begin to scrape it to get fine shavings. The woods that work best are woods that are aromatic, because if it's aromatic it has oils, and if it has oils it's flammable!

How to make an "African man's bag" for your tinder:

You're going to need some quality tinder to help ensure that you always get your fire going. Certain shredded barks and certain leaves make a great tinder. And yes, you *could* carry that tinder around in a paper bag or a plastic bag, but a traditional pouch is so much more traditional and much cooler!

I've long used what's called the African man's bag for my tinder. This is a very simple bag, and very simple to create. I've made most of mine with a piece of scrap leather, but you could use some canvas or cotton from an old garment.

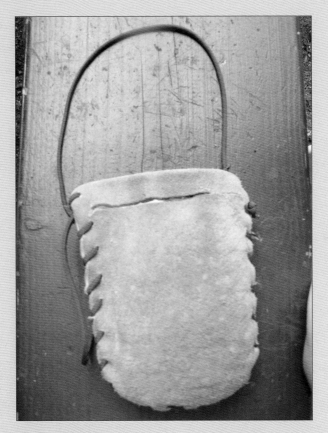

African man's bag.

Look at the picture below to get an idea of the pattern. You first cut the pattern, then cut the slit for the opening, and next sew up the sides. Add a cord for your carrying case and you're done! It's really that simple, and making it will take just as long as it takes for you to sew. You can decorate it, or leave it plain.

It is just a single piece of leather, with no extra pieces for the flap.

I first learned of this style of bag many years ago in an article in the *Wilderness Way* magazine, where the author described this as one of the styles of a nomadic tribe in Africa.

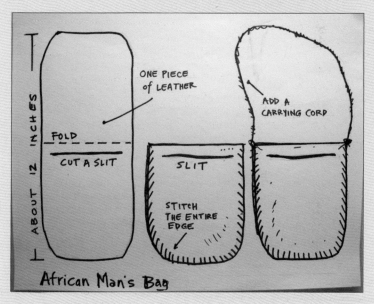

Pattern for man's bag.

Stage two:

Next, wrap your initial birdnest bundle with a slightly bigger bundle, which consists of materials like dry grass, pine needles, shredded bark, and even old newspapers if that's all you have.

Carl blows onto his stage two fire bundle, where the birdnest of mugwort is wrapped with pine needles.

Now you can hold your growing bundle a lot easier, and you can blow into it with a bit more force. Still, not *too* much force, just the right amount. If all is going well, your tinder bundle will be producing increasingly more smoke, and the ember will have grown and spread through the tinder. You can start blowing a bit harder.

Keep blowing on the tinder, and if it's a windy day, all you need to do is to hold the tinder in the wind. Very soon, it will burst into flame. Don't have your face too close—you might lose your eye lashes. Now place your burning bundle into your fire circle.

The excitement of getting the initial coal and working hard to not lose it!

REALITY CHECK

You've got your little flame, but you can't let it go out. Any aromatic leaves, like pine needles, cypress leaves, bay leaves—all these and many more will work. Once, on an overcast day in winter, when it had rained the previous five days and fires seemed impossible, my brother and I stopped at a little bluff by a river in the

Daniela del Valle coaxes her ember to get a flame. *Success! Fire!*

mountains, and hoped to make soup there. We spent the first hour adding tiny little browned pine needles to the flame, and we discovered that dry bay leaves—which were abundant in the area—would burn and sizzle when we added them. So we patiently added those, little by little, until the flame was hot enough to dry out the wet new wood we kept adding. Hikers who walked by stared in disbelief that we actually had a fire, and a few stood around and warmed themselves before moving on.

Scrap bits of plastic can be added at this stage and those recycled hydrocarbon bits burn quite hot and get your fire going. Yes, of course, they are not good for the environment—and nor was the car you drove to the hiking area good for the environment. This is just a life-or-death scenario, where a little burning plastic could be justified. Don't do that on a regular basis.

Stage three:

Now add kindling, the next level of burnable materials. Kindling would consist of little sticks no thicker than pencils, as well as bark, some leaves, and perhaps some pine needles to generate more heat.

You don't want to smother your new fire, so your job is to add kindling and twigs to your fire in such a way that you don't put it out. You create some sort of a fire lay, which refers to the way in which you now pile twigs around the fire so that the fire gets even bigger. You might pile the wood around the fire like a tipi, or a log cabin, or in some other manner.

FIRE LAYS

The fire lay refers to how you're now setting up your twigs to get the fire going. You have your ember, or your flame.

Tipi

Let's consider the so-called tipi fire lay. It's very simple. Lay straight sticks over your little fire, so that they all come to a point in the middle, like a tipi. Once you get a few such sticks laid out, it will be easy to add more and more. The flame licks up and starts to burn the tipi, and you can add more sticks as needed.

Sometimes, a stout vertical stick is pushed into the middle of your fire-to-be, and then the other twigs are leaned onto this central stake. The central stake gives your tipi support.

The Tipi fire lay.

The Log Cabin fire lay.

The Lean-To fire lay.

The Haystack fire lay.

Log Cabin

The log cabin method for getting your fire growing is another option. So you have your little fire in a safe spot. You know what a log cabin looks like, right? Okay, so place bigger twigs around the base of your fire, like a square. Then stack another square of twigs. It's easiest if you do the two opposite ends first, and then lay on the next perpendicular pair. Just keep stacking like that. It helps to define your fire, and it gives your little flame something more to burn. Just keep stacking. As your little log cabin burns, you make another bigger one. Eventually, you'll have a good bed of coals and you can just add logs.

Lean-To

The lean-to fire lay begins with a low tripod of twigs, where two are short and one twig is longer, and then we lean many more twigs and pine needles over the lean-to. The lean-to shape gives the new flame some oxygen, and the new twigs don't smother the flame.

There are many variations of the lean-to lay, such as simply leaning twigs from the edge of your stone fire circle, extending so that the twigs are just above the little flame. These variations are very logical, and yes, children figure this out. You want to create a little space above your new flame, and the lean-to provides support so you can add more twigs.

Haystack

The haystack looks like it sounds, and it means simply laying small dry tinder around and over your little flame, every which way as long as you don't compress too much material at once and smother your flame.

If everything is wet or damp, you'd probably not use this method, because wet conditions require a bit more care to get a good fire going. But under dry conditions, the simple haystack should work fine for getting your fire going.

Now, whatever lay method you use, your job is to continue to build your fire so that a good bed of coals develops. You want a secure fire with hot coals, one that will survive even if it's raining.

Stage four: Time for logs!

Once you've got all your kindling burning well, you should begin to introduce larger material, such as small or large logs. Never take your fire for granted, so when you add wood, keep the principles of the fire lay in mind. Lay in logs so that the flames do not get smothered, and be thoughtful as you continue to add logs to the fire.

What you do from here largely depends on your circumstances, and whether you're building a fire to stay warm, to cook, to dry your clothes, to sit around, to signal, to stay hidden, or some combination of these.

I often like to first frame my initial fire with larger logs, and then I can lay more logs on top, more or less perpendicular to the first logs. This allows for some air space so the fire doesn't get smothered.

REALITY CHECK

When my friend Lee burned an old telephone pole for our campfire.
It was late August, and school would be starting soon, so my friend Lee and I wanted to spend a few days in the forest. We hiked up to Mount Lowe in the

Angeles National Forest, the site of an old resort from a hundred or so years ago. These days, it was all in ruins—just random walls, and stairways leading off to nowhere.

It was quiet and no one else was there that summer night. It was also quite cold, so we knew we needed a fire. Additionally, the entire campsite was remarkably clean of any little brush, as if a Boy Scout troop had spent the entire day cleaning up and removing anything we could burn. But there was an old telephone pole lying off to one side, partially decayed, probably having been replaced years ago for a newer pole.

"We can burn that pole," Lee declared.

"What?" I responded, almost as if getting shocked. "You're going to need lots of small tinder, and there's nothing around to burn," I declared.

"I can do it," was all that Lee said.

He rolled the old pole over to the spot where we wanted our fire, propped up one end of the pole on a thin log—maybe two inches thick, so that it was set perpendicular to the telephone pole. He then proceeded to burn a potato chip bag, and other papers that he had in his pack. It was an old pole, and had once been covered in black creosote as a preservative, and so it was apparently quite flammable. I couldn't believe my eyes as the flames licked into the telephone pole, and Lee somewhere found a few more little twigs and leaned them up to the telephone pole. As the pole burned, he just rolled the pole into the fire as needed.

Amazingly, we had our little fire, and from the coals that continued to drop down, we had enough to cook with and to stay warm.

This is probably not a good idea to try today, because of the many toxic chemicals that have been used as wood preservatives. However, we built this fire around 1970, with a pole that had probably been in the ground fifty years, back before the wood preservatives were as toxic as they are now.

OUTDOOR VS. INDOOR

Getting your initial fire going requires the same steps whether you're building a fire for your wilderness camp, or if you're building a fire in your home fireplace. But then, there are different considerations for each.

Your outdoor fire can be large, big enough for many people to sit around. You're not concerned about the smoke. The sound of popping and cracking adds to the excitement. You could, in many cases, just toss on another log as needed and it will start to burn with the rest of the logs. An outdoor fire can be a bit more wild and unrestrained. Not so with an indoor fire.

An indoor fire is an entirely different matter. The wood to be added must be cut to size in order to fit your fireplace or woodstove. You've got to load the wood into a box or bin so that you're not scattering sawdust and bugs as you bring it into the house. And wood for the home needs to be stored well, so your woodpile is not housing termites, spiders, and even rodents. You need to avoid using resinous wood—like pine—which might suddenly pop and send an ember onto your living room floor. You need to do much more nurturing for an indoor fire, such as watching it more often, making sure the flues are not clogged, and keeping a screen in front of it.

TRANSPORTING THE COAL WHEN TRAVELLING

Before there was a Bic lighter, how did indigenous people carry their embers from place to place? Let's see how it was done.

Since we take the portability of a fire-starting device for granted, most modern people have no idea that once there were many methods for sustaining and carrying an ember which could later be blown into flame.

Through anthropological research of the indigenous peoples of North America, we've learned that tools for making and transporting fire were once quite standard in the people's traveling gear, with many local variations. Most of these skills regarding fire were universal. While the materials might change, the basic techniques have been used all over the world, with slight local and cultural variations.

For transportation of an ember or coal over relatively short distances, you're looking for the same material as you'd use in stage one of getting your ember to a flame. You create a birdnest or a cigar of fine leaves, with a material like dried mugwort. Or you use the shredded inner bark of elder or cedar, which can be shredded and mushed-up into a decent birdnest which will hold the ember and let it smoulder.

Another choice would be using the stalks of certain trees or bushes which have a soft inner pitch. For example, a dried fennel stalk is only about an inch thick, but it can be many feet long. The inner dried pitch is corky, so you can introduce a little ember to this pith, blow on it, and keep it going all day long if necessary.

A stalk or shoot of the elder tree will work similarly. Different species of elder are found world-wide, in nearly all environments. You could use a dried straight shoot of nearly any thickness, though the younger shoots of about an inch thick tend to work the best. Introduce the little ember to one end of the elder, blow on it and the ember will grow into the inner pith of the stick. As long as the day is not rainy and wet, such an ember should survive all day in such a protective covering as the elder shoot.

The dried flower stalks of both yucca and agave have also been used to transport embers, as long as they are no more than a few inches thick. The ideal size for transporting embers would be up to two feet long and perhaps two inches thick. Anything bigger is a bit unwieldly.

Since the outer shell of these flowering stalks is hard, an ember can be introduced into the soft and pithy inside without burning through the shell. It can be relatively easy to introduce an ember and to simply carry it around, starting a new fire when one arrives at camp.

The ability to carry a live coal would have been part of the advanced technology of all indigenous peoples, for it meant that you didn't have to start from scratch to make a fire each time you stopped for the night. It would be akin to the modern urban dweller carrying a Bic lighter everywhere, instead of matches.

TORCHES

Steve Watts, a member of the Society of Primitive Technology, often demonstrated the skills and products of our indigenous past. Watts wrote several books, and frequently contributed to the Society's magazine, the *Bulletin of Primitive Technology*. He described how torches and candles were made in the past, the counterpart to modern flashlights and lanterns.

The torches that Watts made were variable. Some were tight bundles of split bamboo or rivercane, where the end would be lit and used for light. A roll of birchbark was also used, which was tied securely.

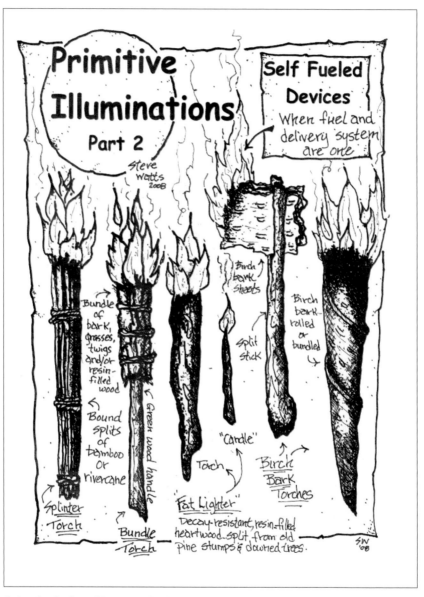

A drawing by Steve Watts on Primitive Illuminations.

Steve Watts teaching how to make a primitive torch at a Rabbit Stick event. Photo courtesy of Dave Wescott.

QUIZ

1. List the four stages of making a fire.
2. Besides mugwort, what's another common material that you could use for carrying an ember?

ANSWERS

1. Finest tinder, larger tinder, kindling, logs.
2. Shredded bark of elder or cedar, laundry lint, fallen birdnests, etc.

ACTION:

Build a little fire in a safe place—even your backyard. Build a tripod over it from long bamboo twigs, and suspend a can from the tripod. Heat enough water for a bowl of soup.

With a hollow piece of bamboo, blow onto the coals of a campfire. Add tinder to the coals, and blow until you get a new flame.

SMOKE SIGNALS

The Fuzz Stick

"Fuzz sticks," pictured below, are ideal fire starters. Use sticks about the thickness of a thumb and about a hand's span long. Cut shavings, but leave the shavings attached to the stick. This is especially useful in wet weather. Try it!

With your knife, carve slivers from the twig so that you end up with a fuzz stick. Don't cut the slivers off completely. Then stack at least three of them, place fine tinder underneath, and start your fire. Drawing by the author.

CHAPTER 5

DIFFERENT FIRES FOR DIFFERENT NEEDS

COOKING

Cooking fires should not be huge. It's too hard to cook something on a huge bonfire. When I first began to attend campouts and backpacking trips organized by Scouts and school groups, there was nearly always a huge bonfire around which everyone sat or stood at night. It was difficult, if not impossible, to cook around such a fire, because it was simply too big and hot to get close enough to easily cook. If you tried to cook on such a fire, as some of my friends did, their food more often than not was burned, and they often got burned too! But everyone always demanded the big round fire because it was the "roundtable" around which everyone talked and laughed and sang.

But meals still needed to be cooked.

When you're ready to cook, it's best to create a small little fire away from the main campfire. (This, of course, assumes that you don't have a Coleman stove or one of the other high-tech cookers available.)

A cooking fire only needs to be big enough to heat the pot of soup or coffee you're trying to warm. In about a minute, a small shallow hole can be dug for your cook fire, measuring perhaps a foot long, and maybe six inches wide. Such a little hollow can be lined with flat rocks, partly to define the fire area, and partly

A tripod is built over a small star fire. Success! Fire!

to create the ledge to rest your pots. By the time a fire is made in such a pit, and burning steadily, one can be ready to cook a meal in as little as ten minutes. (If it has been raining and everything is wet, more time is needed.)

During the many campouts I've gone on from childhood, my outdoor companions and I have built tiny fires like this. Your basic fire setup requires a place

Success! Fire!

to rest the pot—often two bricks or similarly shaped rocks will do—with a fire underneath. Small fires require minimal labor of collecting fuel, and are easy to put out when you're done. In the summer when you don't need the extra heat of the campfire, a small little fire is the way to go.

For a typical campout meal, you often don't need more than one little pot or pan, and maybe two. To cook rice, you need about twenty minutes of good flames, for example.

From the planning perspective, you should look into those foods that require minimal cooking. Most freeze-dried foods only require the addition of hot or boiling water. There are also good camping foods such as instant cereals, potato powder, pre-cooked rice, and meals sold in retort pouches. If you select camping foods that are already cooked, or require minimal cooking, your need for a fire, and the fuel to keep it burning, will be reduced.

DAKOTA PIT

The Dakota pit is made when you dig a hole which goes into the ground vertically for about a foot or so, and a tunnel is dug out which helps to feed oxygen to the fire. You then build your fire in the hole, and place your pot over it. It seems to be a very efficient way to cook and use minimal fuel. If the soil is not too hard, this can be easy and quick to build. You should try it at least once and see if you like it. Where the soil is hard-packed, this method is a bit impractical.

SLEEPING FIRES

When John Muir wandered around Yosemite and through the various mountain ranges of California, he didn't have the advantage of modern-day light-weight camping gear, such as Kelty backpacks and ultra-light sleeping bags.

Muir would find a suitable place to sleep, and then he'd build a huge fire, one as long as his body. If he woke up from the cold, he'd toss a few more logs onto the fire and then go back to sleep. Today, building a fire that large is considered a bit excessive, and if Muir were caught doing it today, he would probably be stripped of his Sierra Club membership, the very organization which he helped found!

Still, if you're in a survival situation, this might be a method that will save your life.

SIGNALLING FIRES

Are fires an option for signaling if you're lost? Yes. Here's how to do it safely.

We know that people in the past used fires—which were typically strategically located on the tops of high peaks—for signaling. For example, in the Anasazi culture of the American Southwest, there is evidence that fires were built at high points which would be seen for twenty miles or more. Craig Childs describes such a system of fire signaling points in his book, *House of Rain*.

But no one really knows how exactly the Anasazi system of signaling actually worked. That is, what were they conveying with their fire signals? Danger? Come help us? The ceremony will begin soon? We don't know.

In today's world, a fire is simply a way of saying, "I am here." If you are lost or stranded, you want someone to know that you are there. Three of anything has long been the international distress signal, so three visible fires is the equivalent of SOS, and you're pleading for help.

There are many possible ways to use signal fires, with whatever code or system you are using worked out and communicated ahead of time. Otherwise, a fire is just a fire!

SMOKEY FIRES

Sometimes you want to be seen if you're lost or hurt. Your fire won't necessarily be seen from great distances, but if you can make a lot of smoke, someone might notice. Build your fire in the open so the smoke won't get dispersed by the trees. If a rescue crew is looking for you, and they see your smoke, it's likely you'll have someone coming in the direction of the fire.

A smokey fire needn't be excessively large, and safety should be your first consideration. The area where you build should be clear of dried grasses and dead undergrowth. It should be in a clearing where there is a chance that the smoke will rise and be seen.

A fire that is burning well with dried material typically produces minimal smoke. To create visible smoke, add green or punky material and more smoke will be produced.

HIDDEN FIRES

Maybe you're in a situation where you need a fire to purify water, or to cook food, or to stay warm, but you really don't want anyone else to see or notice you.

You need to first find a spot where you are somewhat hidden by the natural contours of the land. This might be deep in a narrow canyon, or in a gorge where there are many trees which will serve to diffuse whatever smoke arises. The location could be at the base of an overhang, or in a naturally sheltered section of a deep but dry river bed.

Dig a hole and build a small fire. Make sure all your firewood is dry, and make sure your fire is flaming. Don't use conifers (like pine), which snap and crackle. Find the driest twigs and branches and leaves, and make your fire no bigger than is absolutely necessary for your needs.

If you have to evacuate in a hurry, you can quickly cover your small fire, and be assured that it is safely out.

FIRE IN THE RAIN

Over the years during field trips, my students have made fires so many times, in so many different ways, that we regard it as somewhat routine to make a fire without matches, and we enjoy the special challenge of making a fire in the rain.

When it's raining, it's best to make the fire in an area with natural cover, but that's not always possible. Sometimes, there are very specific areas where you can camp and make fire, and so you just need to adapt to the rain.

Begin by collecting all the firewood and tinder that you can, whether it is wet or dry. The wet material will be on the ground, and the drier material will be dead branches still on the tree, or layers of dead bark still on a standing tree.

You have to create some way so that the rain does not directly fall onto your fire, at least in the early stages.

Here is one method that my students and I have practiced in the past. Pound four upright thick sticks or logs—at least about two feet high—into the ground within the fire pit area, and then place pieces of bark on the top. You have to block some of the rain from your initial fire, or it really is impossible to get a fire going. Once, for the cover, we used a piece of corrugated sheet metal that we found, measuring about three feet by four feet.

Pile up all the wood you've collected nearby. It's a good idea to separate wet from dry wood. Next, produce your ember or a coal from one of the many methods described in this book, and then mother it by adding the tiniest bits of oily pine needles, or eucalyptus bark, and or chip bags, or lint from pockets, or whatever might burn.

The most aromatic leaves are the best because the presence of an aroma means there are lots of oils in those leaves, and that means they will burn well. The early stages of making a fire in the rain are the most critical, so you and your group should huddle around it, keeping the rain out of the early embers with your bodies, and continually adding tiny twigs to the tiny fire.

There is usually plenty of smoke and minimal heat in the early stages of such a fire, because the twigs and branches are drying out. It can take up to an hour to get enough coals under these circumstances so that there is enough heat to start heating water for coffee and heating soup on the side. It could take even longer, depending on the intensity of the rain.

Just kept adding bigger and bigger twigs and branches, and as the little material dries out and burns, you'll be developing a solid bed of coals. If all proceeds well, you might be able to add small- to large-size logs to your fire in about an hour and a half.

If the rain is continuing and getting harder, you will need to create some sort of roof or covering for your fire. This can be bark or layers of logs stacked tipi-style around the large fire. They will burn eventually, and you just keep adding them.

A fire in the rain requires constant attention, especially if the rain grows heavier. One of the most pleasant outdoor experiences you can have is to stand around your warming fire while the rain is coming down upon you. Hopefully, after you dry off and cook, you'll have a shelter to retreat to.

In one case, I was at a campground in the mountains as the rain began. I knew we'd be hiking back out in the rain to our cars a few miles away, and I wanted a warming fire and hot soup before we departed. I was with a dozen students, and Gary Gonzales was working with me. I declared that we were going to make a fire and have soup, and a few students scoffed, telling me that was not possible. Gary just smiled, since we'd done this many times. I asked everyone to help collect a large pile of all possible burnable materials from the area, and though there was some grumbling, everyone proceeded to collect a very large pile of leaves, twigs, logs, and bark. The rain was still light when we began but we still set up our posts and laid a cover of bark pieces on it. We created the fire with magnesium, and initially had only a few eucalyptus leaves burning. A few of the students looked at us with a look of pity, as if we were too stupid to realize that we could not make a fire. At least one man kept stating how it was not possible to make a fire under those conditions.

But we proceeded anyway as the rain got stronger. We had only a small pile of leaves burning, and had to carefully add small twigs, laying them just so, and then nurturing the tiny flame as it got larger and larger. We also had eucalyptus leaves, whose oil content helped to get that little fire going. It took nearly an hour before there were large flames, which we spread around the approximately four-foot-diameter fire circle, so that other twigs and branches could burn as well. Once everyone saw that we actually were going to have a fire, they all crowded closer.

We had already filled two large coffee cans with water from the river, and we added the watercress and other greens we'd collected, along with miso powder. The fire was large and the soup cooked quickly. Everyone warmed up with the delicious soup from the "impossible" fire.

THE VALUE OF A CANDLE

One of my earliest backpacking trips was a high school backpacking trip, accompanied by members of the Sierra Madre Search and Rescue Team. My pack back then was too heavy with food, tools, books, and other junk. But I loved it when we got into our camp for the night.

We backpacked into Spruce Grove, a beautiful little spot tucked away in the folds of the San Gabriel Mountains in the hills above Los Angeles County.

When we were finally getting our fire started for the night's cooking, warmth, and central meeting place, I was having a hard time with my book matches. Abbey Keith of the rescue team came to my rescue, and showed me one of his tricks for getting the campfire going. With a smile, he pulled a fat little pink candle out of his pack and lit it. He used just one match and his candle was lit. Then he stuck that little candle into my damp tinder, and let the wax drip all over the moist sycamore leaves, bay leaves, and pine needles. Lo and behold, the tinder continued to burn. And burn. And the little flame dried out the other tinder. Abbey moved the candle to the opposite side of the fire and did the same, creating a hot spot there, too. He told me to nurture the spot by carefully laying pine needles all around its perimeter, and then adding little twigs, which quickly dried out. We continued this way, working on building up this fire as if it were the most important task in the world.

That fire provided us with plenty of warmth, coals for cooking, and the focal point as we sat around it and talked into the night. And I never forgot Abbey Keith's suggestion of the little candle in the pack to save on your matches.

QUIZ

1.   John Muir would probably be excommunicated from the very Sierra Club he helped to found. Why?
2.   Why did the Anasazi create signaling fires that could be seen for twenty-plus miles?
3.   How do you make your fire smokey if you need the smoke for signaling?

ANSWERS

1.   Often not carrying sleeping gear, Muir would build a huge fire near where he slept. He'd just toss more wood onto the fire if he got cold.
2.   No one knows!
3.   You can smoulder it with too much wood, or add wet and punky material such as grass and wet vegetation.

ACTION:

Set up two bricks, just big enough to straddle a can or pot between them. Build a very small fire and use only dry twigs. Heat up at least two cups of water, enough for hot tea for yourself and your friend.

SMOKE SIGNALS:

"Isn't it interesting that primitive people sweated to make fires and took great pains to keep sparks or embers alive, and now, modern man toils to put out fires?"—*A Primer of Ecological Principles*, Richard J. Vogl

CHAPTER 6

BRINGING THE FIRE INDOORS

You're not always going to be in the woods, are you? Still, if you have a fireplace in your home, it can be one of the most economical ways to heat your home, and even cook your food in an emergency.

In the outdoors, you don't need the same finesse at making your fires as you need indoors. At home, you don't want a wood that crackles and pops like that popular cereal, shooting hot embers into your room! Burning your house to the ground is much worse than burning down your little outdoor lean-to!

When you're bringing your fire into your home, you're going to be using a built-in fireplace, a free-standing fireplace, or a woodstove. Those are your primary options.

FIREPLACE

Fireplaces are notoriously inefficient. There are a few modifications that can be done to increase the heating quotient of your fireplace. The easiest modification is to obtain a grill made from hollow tubes. In theory, when you're burning wood in your fireplace with one of these grills, the cooler air is drawn into the lower part of the tubes, and then hotter air comes out the top into your room. Depending on the layout of the room, as well as other factors, most people find at least a 10 percent increase in the ability of the fire to heat the room when using these grills.

Some of these grills have been manufactured with little fans that blow the hot air into your room. These are a significant improvement over the hollow grills alone.

Typically, the fireplace has a single vertical flue, and most of the gases are simply lost to the atmosphere. Sometimes, bafflings can be added to slow down the loss of gases and improve the ability of the fireplace to heat your room.

The Russian fireplace is a style of building the flue so that there is a series of baffles, meaning heat and gases from the fireplace do not simply exit vertically. The Russian fireplace requires more space to build, as the flue goes back and forth several times before it opens to your chimney. In the process, a larger mass of brick is heated, which further warms your room. (Plans for the Russian fireplace can be obtained from building supply businesses or online.)

FREESTANDING FIREPLACE

These can be sheet metal or cast iron. Since you're installing one of these, you need to find the most efficient place in your room to place it. It must be at least eighteen inches away from any wall, and you need to place it on a fireproof surface.

When you shop around for one of these, you'd do well to find one which also has a flat top surface that can be used for some cooking.

Sheet metal is cheaper and weighs less, so it's easier to manipulate into place. But, sections of it will burn out in time and will need to be repaired or replaced. Cast iron is typically more expensive, weighs a lot more, and can last nearly forever if properly cared for. There are *many* options to choose from in cast iron woodstoves, so look at the various manufacturers' catalogs to find the features you want.

If you're sure you only want a unit to heat your place, it will be a simple matter to find a fireplace that suits your needs. If you want to add the possibility of cooking to the fireplace, then your options are more complex.

Be sure to investigate the used market when looking for a fireplace or woodstove.

The vent tubing required to get the smoke out of your living room and to the outside can be purchased at most building supply centers. Be sure to learn of the local building codes which apply to woodstoves and wood fireplaces. These codes are meant to protect you and keep your home from burning to the ground. For example, you must have a triple-walled flue where it comes in contact with your ceiling and roof. You do not want to try to save money there. And the top of the flue outside your house must be above the top-most point of your roof. These and other guidelines are readily available from local Building and Safety departments of most cities.

Another consideration for getting the most heat from your freestanding fireplace is the placement of your venting tubes. Though you could just have a vent that goes vertically to the outside, you'd trap more heat if you put a few angles in your venting.

One of the easiest methods I've seen is to bring the tubing up vertically, nearly to the ceiling, and then run a line horizontally a few feet before it then goes vertical and out through your roof. That horizontal line of tubing will capture a lot of otherwise wasted heat and deliver it to your room.

WOODSTOVE

There are the same considerations for the woodstove as there are for the free-standing fireplace.

However, you need to be even more meticulous when it comes to safety because you're likely to be using a woodstove every day for your cooking.

Make sure you have proper clearances around the woodstove, and that your flues are cleaned at least once a year. Make sure you empty your ash box regularly.

A WOOD RACK FOR STACKING/STORING YOUR WOOD

If you're using wood for heat or cooking, you have to find a neat, tidy, clean, and dry place outside to store it, and you need to watch it to make sure it doesn't develop termites, black widow nests, or squirrel nests.

Lumber yards and building supply stores sell simple racks for stacking your firewood conveniently. These are well worth it, and make your use of firewood much more convenient.

A rack can also be made quite simply with 2x4s. Your goal is to have a dedicated space to store wood so that it is off the ground, where wood can be stored perhaps up to five feet high. If you build your own rack, the base can be 2x4s set on end for the length of the rack, with shorter 2x4s cut for the depth of the rack. Each end of the rack consists of well-secured 2x4s which are as high as you want to stack the wood. A few 2x4s should also be screwed in to define a top area. This gives your wood rack stability and it allows you to throw a cover over your wood pile in the event of rain.

Keep your wood pile clean and covered if necessary. You don't want animals living there if the wood pile hasn't been touched for several months.

GATHERING WOOD

Are you intending to purchase your firewood, or do you want to gather it yourself, hopefully for as cheaply as possible?

Tree pruners and arborists cut down trees constantly, and they then need to dispose of that wood. Sometimes, they have an arrangement with a wood lot, who will trim it to size and sell it back to the consumer.

Sometimes, the wood is simply chipped and used as mulch, or unceremoniously taken to the local city dump. One of your best choices for getting free or low-cost firewood is to locate some of the arborists in your area, and arrange to go pick up some of their wood, or have it delivered. You might be surprised how easily this can be done, because they typically have to pay to dispose of it. The key is timing! You may have to be willing to rush to a tree-pruning site on short notice in order to take advantage of obtaining wood.

Another option is to grow trees and shrubs whose trimmings you can cut, dry, and use for your own fireplace. Most people do this already in rural areas, where there is no shortage of firewood. But even in urban areas, trees are constantly being pruned of their dead wood, and trees are constantly being cut down. In order to get a notice of when trees in your area are being cut down, you'd need to talk to arborists in your area, and notify friends that you're always on the alert for firewood.

For home use, you shouldn't need a chain saw to reduce your wood to fireplace size. You should be discriminating when you first select wood, and don't take logs that are too big to handle. Select logs that you can roll into your truck, and then roll back out to your splitting and stacking area.

WOOD SELECTION

The two mostly widely planted trees in the world are pine and eucalyptus, which are mostly used for the lumber trade. Both of these trees are widely planted in North America for landscaping purposes. This means that their branches are commonly pruned, and available at wood lots or city pruning lots, sometimes for free.

In terms of ideal wood selection, hardwoods are best. Look at Appendix 2 for the relative BTU content of the different trees of North America. This will help you choose the best woods for your situation, whether you buy your wood or collect it for free.

Pines are best avoided in your fireplace, except perhaps when starting the fire. Their oil content causes them to burn very hot, and often crack and pop erratically as hot embers fly about.

Some of the so-called "junk trees"—those trees which grow like weeds—typically have a lower BTU content and burn up quickly. Such trees include tree of heaven, elm, and ash.

Keep in mind that your selection of wood is a very personal matter, often dictated by your budget, and local availability of woods. And since *any* wood can be burned, my policy is to rarely turn down any wood that's free.

GETTING FREE WOOD

When I lived in Northeast Los Angeles, I was not that concerned about wood selection. My priority was that I did not want to pay for wood, especially when there was so much available for free. Each Tuesday on trash pickup day, I drove around town and found that other neighbors pruned their various trees, and actually bundled it up for the trash collector to take away. Not only that, they often pruned it into convenient lengths for the trash pickup, which was also a convenient length for my woodstove.

Sometimes neighbors would have a tree cut down and the large pieces would be there by the street, waiting several days for some crew to haul it away to the dump. I would often take these pieces—usually pine or eucalyptus—and stack them in my firewood pile to dry and season. Then, when I needed them, I had to go out with my heavy maul and split the wood into pieces that would fit into the woodstove or fireplace. It was hard work, but very enjoyable.

WHAT'S THE BEST WOOD?

What's the best wood for your fireplace? Numerous studies have been done over the years by different organizations to determine which woods make the best logs in your fireplace. In general, it all comes down to the wood's rating in BTUs—British Thermal Units. More BTU means the hotter or longer your fire will burn. Less BTU means that you have some inexpensive wood that will burn up quickly and provide you with a minimal heat—that's why certain wood on the wood lot is very cheap, and other wood—like oak—is very expensive.

WHAT'S A BTU!?
BTUs, or British Thermal Units, are a measure of the amount of heat energy available in any given substance. All firewood has about the same BTU per pound. Non-resinous wood has around 8000 to 8500 BTU per pound, and

resinous wood has around 8600 to 9700 BTU per pound. Less dense softwoods have less BTU per cord than more dense hardwood but they also weigh less per cord. Resinous wood has more BTU per pound because the resins have more BTU per pound than wood fiber has.

See Appendix 2 to compare the BTU content of different woods.

THE SLUSH LAMP FOR LIGHTING

If you don't have electric lights, there are several traditional methods for bringing lighting into your home. These include candles, fuel gas lanterns, battery lanterns, and solar lanterns. Much has been written about each of these options, in magazines such as *Mother Earth News*, *American Survival Guide*, and others. Whole books have been written about how to light your home using state-of-the-art lanterns, such as Aladdins. We recommend that you look into these great modern devices, and purchase lanterns for daily use or emergencies.

The slush lamp is another option that goes back millennia. It's easier to make than even a candle!

Remember the traditional oil lamps of the Middle East, as in the story of Hanukkah? The little oil lamps were probably clay, filled with oil, and contained a little wick which extended beyond the oil. These have been around for millennia and are easy to make when you need a quick emergency candle or heater.

We've made them with metal jar lids, glass baby food jar, half-coconut shells, metal cups, and anything that will hold oil. You can use any oil—cheap oil, quality olive oil, or anything in between. All will burn. The wick can be an actual candle wick, a twisted piece of cotton, or a rolled up piece of mullein leaf.

The hardest part can be getting the wick to stand up straight in the oil.

Here's a method that I was taught by Alan Halcon during one of our Dirttime events. First, Alan poured some cooking oil into a small glass jar, roughly the size of a baby food jar. Then he took a wine cork and cut a round piece from it, about a third of an inch thick. Then, he carved a little hole in the middle of the cork, and slipped a candle wick through it. Most of the wick was in the bottom part and the top part of the cork had only a small portion extending.

Alan Halcon cuts a slice from a wine cork.

After cutting a hole into the middle of the cork, Halcon inserts a wick.

The cork floats in a baby food jar that has been filled with oil, making a simple slush lamp.

He placed the wick in the oil, and it floated there. He lit the wick, and it burned well. Since the cork floated, it gradually descended as the oil was used up. Alan said that he had some of these which burned for many hours.

QUIZ

1. What are the two most widely planted trees in the world?
2. The modern fireplace is one of the most efficient ways to heat your home. True or false.

ANSWERS

1. Pine and Eucalyptus.
2. False. They are notoriously inefficient, with most of the heat going up the chimney.

ACTION:

Take some time and make a little slush lamp. Just make a simple one in a little container with oil.

SMOKE SIGNALS:

"The fire is of the first importance. Start it with fine kindling and clean, dry, hemlock bark. When you have a bright, even fire from end to end of the space, keep it up with small fagots of the sweetest and most wholesome woods of the forest. These are, in the order named, black birch, hickory, sugar maple, yellow birch, and red beech. The sticks should be short, and not over two inches across. Split wood is better than round. The outdoor range can be made by one man in little more than an hour, and the camper-out, who once tries it, will never wish to see a 'portable camp-stove' again."—*Woodcraft and Camping*, Nessmuk

CHAPTER 7

FIRE SAFETY AND ECOLOGY

SAFETY

Remember, you want to enjoy the solitude of the woods, be safe, and not cause a forest fire. Here are the precautions you should always practice.

Always clear an area near your camp before you start making a fire. Make sure there are no low-hanging branches that might catch fire.

A smaller fire is easier to manage than a big fire. Try to avoid oily-poppy wood, like pine, which can send out hot embers many feet from the campfire.

Be sure that someone is always watching your active campfire. Don't be one of those guys who wanders off and just leaves the fire.

Once there was a popular slogan by Smokey the Bear: "Remember, only YOU can prevent forest fires." Fires in the forest are generally regarded as a bad thing, especially if your home is about to go up in flames. So the policy has been to suppress fires. No one wants to lose their home—or their neighborhood! On the other hand, fire is often the main factor that has shaped and controlled various landscapes throughout the world—such as the Great Plains, the Australian outback, and much of Southern California. Many plants do not sprout up except after a fire. Fire is not a bad thing. It just *is*.

Scouts and family being mentored in the safe use of fire.

Still, no one wants your home, or your entire neighborhood, to be burned to the ground. If you need a fire, you must practice the personal responsibility of keeping it under your control.

On the flip side, indigenous people have long used fire as a method of agriculture.

According to M. Kat Anderson, author of *Tending the Wild: Native American Knowledge and the Management of California's Natural Resources*, "Fire was the most significant, effective, efficient, and widely employed vegetation management tool of California Indian tribes."

She continues, "Deliberate burning increased the abundance and density of edible tubers, greens, fruits, seeds, and mushrooms; enhanced feed for wildlife; controlled the insects and diseases that could damage wild foods and basketry material; increased the quantity and quality of material used for basketry and cordage; and encouraged the sprouts used for making household items, granaries, fish weirs, clothing, games, hunting and fishing traps, and weapons. It also removed dead material and promoted growth through the recycling of nutrients, decreased plant competition, and maintained specific plant community types such as coastal prairies and montane meadows."

These comments are generally applicable to other areas in the world where fire was used as a tool of passive agriculture.

SMOKE SIGNALS:

"Many Aboriginal peoples are very aware of the right time of year and correct ways of using a fire. The frequency of burning and the time of year are chosen by the impact this approach has on food supplies and other survival factors. The overall effect of these fires is called 'fire-stick farming,' and it has created a light, regular mosaic pattern of burning, producing neighboring habitats at different stages of regeneration after fire."—*Fire Making: The Forgotten Art*, Daniel Hume

EPILOGUE

Fire. Is it a creative or a destructive force? Is it a thing or a process? Does it have "life," as some metaphysicians have suggested?

Much to ponder . . . .

Now that you know fire just a little better, and hopefully can produce a fire even if there were no more matches, here are some of the things you can do:

- Cook food
- Make soup
- Purify water

- Create tools
- Signal long distances
- Stay warm

- Burn wastes
- Create ash and charcoal for other uses
- Destroy vermin

- Have light
- Have insight
- Stay alive!

Have you talked to your fire today?

TEST YOUR FIRE SKILLS

1. ☐ TRUE. ☐ FALSE. There is little statistical evidence to show that the skill of primitive fire-starting has ever saved anyone's life.

2. ☐ TRUE. ☐ FALSE. Modern "strike-anywhere" wooden matches and a butane lighter are really all the fire-starting tools that a wilderness traveler needs.

3. ☐ TRUE. ☐ FALSE. Thanks to space age technology, the need for matches (and all other "old" fire starting methods) will be virtually obsolete within ten years.

4. ☐ TRUE. ☐ FALSE. The Indian bow and drill, which produced fire by the friction of a drill onto a baseplate, is a difficult, inefficient way to start a fire, and thus this method has never been widely practiced.

5. ☐ TRUE. ☐ FALSE. The oldest, most popular historical method of fire-starting was simply rubbing two pencil-shaped sticks together.

6. Your car stalls in the cold high country. How can you start a fire, using only those items which are on, or part of, the car? List two possibly methods.
   1._____
   2._____

7. The fastest recorded speed for producing a fire with the bow-and-drill was _____.

8. Success in using the bow and drill for fire depends on, essentially, two factors:
   1._____
   2._____

9. Using the bow and drill method for fire starting necessitates being able to find appropriate pieces of wood, and a thong. Since the thong may be the most difficult component to find, or fabricate, from nature, name at least two sources for a thong from your clothing, parts of your clothing, or something that you're likely wearing.

   1._____

   2._____

10. Concentrating or focusing on the sun's rays to a point is a simple fire-starting method that any child can do. List at least five manmade devices that can be used for this purpose, and at least one natural item:

    1._____ 2._____ 3._____

    4._____ 5._____

    Natural: _____

11. List two ways to start fire with your flashlight

    1._____ 2._____

12. [For hunters] Lacking a conventional fire-starting method, how can you start a fire? You only have your shotgun, ammo, and the clothing you're wearing.

13. List five wilderness tinders:

    1._____ 2._____ 3._____

    4._____ 5._____

14. List five manmade tinders you're likely to find in the wilderness:

    1._____ 2._____ 3._____

    4._____ 5._____

15. A punk in any material that will slowly smolder without actually bursting into flames. Of what value is such a material in the wilderness?

16. List at least three punk materials:

    1._____   **2.**_____   **3.**_____

17. List the three basic stages in building a campfire:

    1._____   **2.**_____   **3.**_____

18. Which of the camper's positions (below) provides the maximum benefits from the fire? State why.

A. The Fire is between the camper and the wall. B. The camper is between the fire and the wall. Which is better? Drawing by the author.

19. When cooking over an open fire, coals are best for _____ and flames are best for _____. (State a type of cooking for each.)

20. Generally speaking, which is more efficient for cooking: a "round" campfire, or a "long" (roughly rectangular) campfire? State why.

21. Which provides the most warmth:
    1. Sleeping with your head facing your fire;
    2. Sleeping with your feet facing your fire; or
    3. Sleeping so that your entire body is alongside the fire.

22. Save your energy! Instead of chopping a large log in two (with the risk of splinters in your eyes and your fingers chopped), _____ _____. (State what you would do)

23. A fire blower is a hollow tube for stirring up dead fires. It is used to fan air directly on any coals that may still be live. One can be from any hollow stem, such as _____. (List type of plants).

24. Fire is an essential tool of survival. List at least five of its functions:

    1._____   2._____   3._____

    4._____   5._____

APPENDIX 1

ANSWERS TO FIRE QUIZ

1. False. This is one of the critical skills that has enabled people in survival situations to be survivors and not statistics.

2. False. Matches can get wet, or be used up. A butane light can likewise be used up. Primitive methods are an extremely valuable back-up.

3. False. Even if this were true, you'd still need to carry those space-age devices, whatever they may be. In the absence of devices, we should know how to make fire using the simplest of components from nature.

4. False. The bow and drill, and its many variations, have been used for millennia by peoples of past ages who had no steel, or had limited knowledge of chemicals. Though it may seem difficult and inefficient at first attempt, it becomes easier with practice.

5. False. Cartoons frequently depict an American Indian or Boy Scout rubbing two pencil-shaped sticks together. In fact, one vertical stick—the drill – is spun onto a base plate with a small bow. See the illustration.

6. 1) The cigarette lighter. 2) The battery and jumper cables. Attach jumper cables to the battery, and then clip a piece of wire (about four inches or so) to one of the free cables. Wrap some tinder onto the wire. Take the other free cable and touch it to the wire. An electric arc will pass through the wire—it will glow red—and quickly ignite the tinder. This is potentially dangerous since batteries may explode. It is best done by removing the battery from the car, and attempting to make fire as far away from the car as possible. 3) The reflector around the headlight. Open up the headlight and remove the reflector. Insert tinder into the light bulb opening, and point at the sun. The reflector focuses the sun light onto the tinder and ignites it. Newer model cars may have headlights which are more difficult to open. 4) Your road

flares. There are other methods of getting a fire from various parts of your car and engine. Most are potentially hazardous and should not be attempted by someone inexperienced in the workings of engines. For that reason, they are not included here.

7. In a Boy Scout competition, a record was set at 6.4 seconds. The Scout was in position to drill when the clock started, and he produced a flame in that short time. Obviously, his tools were the most ideal, and he had practiced a lot. Most folks don't even get a book of matches open in 6.4 seconds. Primitive fire technician Alan Halcon has produced an ember in two seconds with the hand drill, described in this book.

8. The quality of the fire-making components, and your level of skill.

9. There are many possibilities for thong (bow-string) material: shoestring, camera strap, a belt, the elastic waste of underwear, a brassier strap, the seam of various garments, a tie, etc.

10. Manmade devices: magnifying glass, binoculars, rifle scope, Fresnel lens, camera lens, some prescription eyeglasses, and others.
    Natural method: Ice. Large flat pieces of clear ice, approximately five feet in diameter, have been used by Inuits. One surface of the ice is first carved into concavity in order to create a lens. The ice is stood upright, and—if properly made—will focus sunlight onto tinder about six feet away.

11. The first method involves removing the reflector around the bulb. Place tinder into the hole, and point the reflector at the sun. Tinder ignites quickly on sunny days, and may take less time when the sun is low in the sky. The second method involves removing the batteries, and requires some fine steel wool. This can be done with two C cells, but is easier with at least two D cells. You hold the two batteries together in correct alignment (as they'd be in the flashlight). Then you stretch the steel wool from the top of the cell, down to the bottom. As the electric current passes through the steel wool, the steel wool heats up and finally glows red. At that stage, you introduce tinder into the steel wool and blow on it until you get your flames.

12. This must be done very carefully. First, open up one shell. Modern plastic shells may be difficult to open and you will probably have to cut off the top. Remove the shot, and the plastic wadding. Leave the powder intact. Insert

a small piece of cotton clothing or kerchief. Now close the shell. In an open area, fire the round either up into the air or into a sandy area where there is no chance of spreading a fire. The cotton should be burning or smoldering. Quickly add tinder and blow to a flame.

13. Dried cattail spikes, dried mugwort (*Artemisia sp.*) leaves, dried and pulverized sagebrush leaves (*Artemisia tridentata*), dried pine needles, dried bay leaves, dried and pulverized grass, bird nests, dried moss, certain animal hairs, etc.

14. Old newspapers, old cardboard boxes, mattress stuffing, stuffing from old car seats, old cotton clothing, etc.

15. In the pre-steel days particularly, indigenous peoples used large cigar-shaped punks to carry a live coal from camp to camp so they could easily start a fire at the next camp. Campers can employ this same method to save on matches (assuming you have any).

16. Dried mugwort leaves and sagebrush stems are ideal. Other possibilities include the stems of plants with a dry pith which easily holds a coal, such as elder, fennel, or yucca. Other possibilities include ground up bark and leaves which have been rolled up into a large cigar-shape.

17. Tinder, kindling, and large fuel logs. Though there isn't always a crisp distinction between these stages, the point is to start by burning the smallest materials, gradually adding larger materials, and finally burning logs. I've built large fires in the rain by following this procedure.

18. Position B is better because the camper has the rock on one side, and the fire on the other. As the night progresses, the rocks will absorb heat, and they'll radiate that heat throughout the night. The camper will then have the warm cliff on one side, and the coals on the other.

19. Coals are best for baking and slow cooking—which is how all food should be prepared to preserve the most nutrient. Flames are used for boiling water, or for frying and broiling.

20. A long campfire is much more efficient than a large round one. A long fire requires a lot less wood, pots can be straddled across the fire by rocks on both sides, and—because of less heat—you can sit closer to prepare your meal. After the cooking is done, many people prefer large round fire to sit around and talk.

21. Sleeping with your entire body alongside the fire will provide the most warmth, which is another reason why a long camp fire is preferred. However, if you're with a group and have chosen to have only one fire, you may not have the luxury of sleeping this way.

22. Burn the log in two. This is easier than you may think. Heavy axes are rarely needed in the wilderness.

23. Elder, fennel, various grasses, and reeds.

24. Fire is used to purify water, for warmth, for signaling, to cook foods, for hot water for proper physical hygiene, for fire-hardening tools, for protection, for light, etc.

APPENDIX 2

FIREWOOD BTU RATING CHARTS
FOR COMMON TREE SPECIES

The firewood BTU rating charts below give a comparison between different hardwoods and softwoods. This can help you decide what the best firewood type is for your needs.

Trees are organized by highest BTU first. Numbers are from California Energy Commission, Firewood Resources, and other sources. BTU ratings are based on ninety cubic feet of solid wood per 128 cubic foot cord.

A cord is 128 cubic feet of stacked wood. Because of the air space between the pieces of wood, the amount of solid wood in a cord may be only seventy to ninety cubic feet, even though the volume of the stack is 128 cubic feet.

With most BTU charts, there are sometimes differences in the numbers, though most seem to be pretty close. Much of the inconsistencies are from different variables such as how much actual solid wood is assumed to be in a cord. A cord is 128 cubic feet, but in any stack of wood there will be air space between the pieces. As a result, a "cord" of wood could have as little as seventy cubic feet of actual solid wood. This varies with the size and shape of the wood and how tightly it is stacked.

Species	Heat content: million BTUs per cord	Weight: pounds per cord, dried
Live oak	36.6	4,840
Eucalyptus	34.5	4,560
Almond	32.9	4,350
Osage orange	32.9	4,728
Pacific madrone	30.9	4,086
Dogwood	30.4	4,025

Species	Heat content: million BTUs per cord	Weight: pounds per cord, dried
Oregon white oak	28.0	3,710
Shagbark hickory	27.7	4,327
Calif. Black oak	27.4	3,625
Pinyon Pine	27.1	
Black birch	26.8	3,890
Black locust	26.8	3,890
Bitternut hickory	26.5	3,832
Honey locust	26.5	4,100
Apple	25.8	3,712
Mulberry	25.7	4,012
Northern red oak	24.0	3,757
Sugar maple	24.0	3,757
White oak	24.0	3,757
White ash	23.6	3,689
Lodgepole pine	22.3	2,580
Red elm	21.6	3,112
Black walnut	20.0	3,120
Sugar pine	19.6	2,270
Sycamore	19.1	2,992
Willow	14.3	2,236
Cottonwood	13.5	2,108

WORKS CITED

Outdoor Survival Skills, Larry Dean Olsen

Survival Skills of Native California, Paul Campbell

Fire Making: The Forgotten Art of Conjuring Flame with Spark, Tinder, and Skill,
   Daniel Hume

How to Survive Anywhere, Christopher Nyerges

INDEX

ABOUT THE AUTHOR

Christopher Nyerges has been teaching ethno-botany and survival skills since 1974. He has worked with numerous organizations over the years and co-founded the School of Self-Reliance. He has authored numerous books on survival and self-reliance. He resides in Southern California. He can be contacted at www.SchoolofSelf-Reliance.com.